D0198670

Interpreting the Bible

A *Popular Introduction*
to Biblical Hermeneutics

by

Terence J. Keegan, O.P.

Please return our book so that
others can enjoy it too. Thanks

Mother Cabrini Shrine

201 Cabrini Blvd.

Golden, CO

303-526-0758

PAULIST PRESS
New York, N.Y./Mahwah, N.J.

Copyright © 1985
by Terence J. Keegan, O.P.

All rights reserved. No part of this book may be reproduced or transmitted in any form or by any means, electronic or mechanical, including photocopying, recording or by any information storage and retrieval system without permission in writing from the Publisher.

Library of Congress
Catalog Card Number: 85-61737

ISBN: 0-8091-2747-4

Published by Paulist Press
997 Macarthur Boulevard
Mahwah, New Jersey 07430

Printed and bound in the
United States of America

CONTENTS

PREFACE

The main content of this book was first presented in a series of five lectures in June 1984 at the annual theological colloquium sponsored by the Graduate Program in Religious and Biblical Studies at Providence College, Providence, Rhode Island. The purpose of these colloquia is to provide the participants with an opportunity to remain abreast of recent scholarly developments. The focus of my five lectures was somewhat unusual since it was more on methodology than on content. I chose this focus because over the past two decades a number of new methodologies have been introduced into the study of Scripture, methodologies that are too often understood only by those who are proficient in them.

My own attempts at understanding and utilizing these new methodologies had led me to recognize the importance of several of them for the relationship between scholars and the Church. The potential impact of these newer methodologies, however, would never be realized unless there was a more general understanding and appreciation of their nature and value. The lectures, delivered to an audience of educators, preachers and others involved in Church ministry, were very well received and I was encouraged to make the substance of these lectures available to a wider audience.

This book, a revision and expansion of these lectures, deals primarily with three recent methodologies, structuralism, reader-response criticism and canonical criticism. It is intended

1

to make these methodologies more understandable and accessible to the ordinary student of the Bible.

The emergence of these new methods is first set in perspective by a consideration of interpretive methodologies that have been used throughout the history of the Church. Not only have new methods been appearing with regularity but these methods, both past and present, have invariably been developed from methods first used in secular studies. Being derived from secular studies, biblical methodologies are often based on philosophical presuppositions. Each of the new methods is, therefore, considered in the light of its presuppositions as well as in terms of the benefits that can be derived from its use.

Until recently the dominant method in use by biblical scholars has been the historical-critical method. One chapter is therefore devoted to a comparison of the historical-critical method with these newer methodologies. Subsequent chapters give individual treatment to each of the new methods. Each of the methods is explained in detail, exemplified with biblical passages and illustrated with charts and diagrams. The use of technical terminology was unavoidable but a glossary at the end of the book is provided as a helpful reference.

The publication of this book gives me an opportunity to acknowledge my indebtedness to a number of people. The Rev. Cyril Dettling, O.P., the coordinator of the theological colloquium, made the original lecture presentation possible and encouraged my continuing work. The members of the Catholic Biblical Association's task force on the narrative criticism of Matthew's Gospel stimulated my interest in and deepened my appreciation of recently developed methodologies. I would also like to thank the Rev. Lawrence Boadt, C.S.P. of Paulist Press for his encouragement and editorial assistance. Finally, special thanks are due to Mr. Stephen Dalton, my graduate assistant, not only for numerous helpful suggestions but also for countless hours of tedious work in preparing the manuscript for publication.

Terence J. Keegan, O.P.
Providence College
Providence, Rhode Island

Chapter 1

THE NATURE OF BIBLICAL HERMENEUTICS

Hermeneutics, in any field of inquiry, is concerned with interpretation. Biblical hermeneutics is concerned with methods for interpreting the text of the Bible. During the past two decades there have been a number of developments in the study of the Bible that could significantly alter the view of scholars about what the Bible is and how it is to be interpreted. The full impact of these developments has yet to be felt among biblical scholars generally, and some of them are, in fact, meeting with resistance. It is the contention of this book, however, that these new developments are actually moving biblical scholarship in the direction of a more ancient understanding of what the Bible is and, more importantly, in the direction of a more ancient understanding of the proper relationship between biblical scholarship and the community of believers, the Church.

1. BIBLICAL INTERPRETATION AND BIBLICAL CRITICISM

Biblical interpretation and biblical criticism are closely related and often confused. Their relationship and distinction can perhaps be illustrated by the present author's experience with two distinct works of criticism. In the spring of 1984 I came across two seemingly unrelated writings. One was a book by Leo Steinberg entitled *The Sexuality of Christ in Renaissance Art and in Modern Oblivion* (N.Y.: Pantheon, 1983); the other was a newspaper article by Robert Hilburn on the rock music of Bruce Springsteen ("Boss's Memo," *Providence Journal Bulletin*, June 10, 1984, pp. H-13, 15). Both of these items fascinated me because each was able to explain aspects of forms of art that I had thus far failed to appreciate. Why did Renaissance artists depict Jesus' genital organs? How did this depiction enhance the overall effect of their works of art? What was the intended overall effect? Why did later Christian artists stop depicting Jesus' genital organs? Steinberg answers these questions in such a clear and convincing fashion that my appreciation of Renaissance art has been significantly enhanced. Some of Steinberg's answers will be used to illustrate the discussion in Chapter IX on the Bible in the Church today.

While I have long appreciated Renaissance art and have had some understanding of it, I cannot say the same for rock music. Nevertheless, the article on Bruce Springsteen attracted my attention because the only rock concert I had ever attended was one given by Bruce Springsteen. My attendance at this concert was part of a short-lived attempt to understand the music enjoyed by my college students, an attempt which failed. I went to the concert but was unable to understand why or how it was that these students were so appreciative of what was going on. The article by Hilburn, however, was impressive because it was an attempt to explain what is going on in the rock music of Bruce Springsteen. Criticism of any kind is an attempt to explain. This critical article probed what was going on in Springsteen's album, *Born in the U.S.A.*, and tried to explain how and why the music of Springsteen has the effect that it does have on its listeners. The article, however, went beyond an analysis of how the album communicated to a discussion of its message. According to this article, one of the messages that Springsteen is attempting to convey in his album is that "the absence of hope blurs the distinction between freedom and captivity." The album, it seems, is trying to communicate something quite profound, at least in the view of the critic, Robert Hilburn.

What do studies on rock music and Renaissance painting have to do with biblical interpretation? The answer is that both of these studies represent attempts to explain what is going on in a particular form of art. That is precisely what biblical interpretation does, i.e., attempts to explain what is going on in the Bible. The work of biblical scholars is actually quite similar to the work of literary critics or art critics or music critics. The fact that the work of biblical scholars is often referred to as biblical criticism underscores its fundamental similarity with the criticism practiced in more secular disciplines. The critical methods used in biblical studies are actually derived from methods first used by critics in music, art and especially literature. The new developments to be considered in this book, especially structuralism and reader-response criticism, involve methods which have been derived from approaches recently developed for use in the study of secular literature. These methods are somewhat at odds with the historical-critical method which up to the present has been the dominant if not the exclusive method used in biblical studies. The fact of the matter is, however, that the historical-critical method was itself derived from methodologies first used in secular studies.

Biblical scholars actually perform two related but distinct functions. One function is to interpret the biblical text in order to assist the believing community in appreciating what it is that the biblical text is saying. The other function is more fundamental—it is to determine how the biblical text has the effect it does or should have in the believing community. It is one thing to determine how or why a given art form has the effect it does have on its audience. It is quite another thing to determine the meaning of a particular work of art. The work of criticism is primarily concerned with the former function, though critics often serve their own audiences' needs by performing the second function as well. Though biblical critics often seem more concerned with determining the meaning of a text, this interpretive function of scholars could not be performed without first determining how and why the text has the effect it does have. The new methodologies to be discussed in this book all have the virtue of being quite explicit about the critical basis of their interpretive work.

2. CRITICS AND READERS

Criticism seeks to determine how something does what it does and often passes judgment on whether it does this well or badly. Art critics, movie critics and biblical critics all seek to determine how a given work produces the effects that it does produce. A wide variety of methods have been developed in various disciplines that enable the critics to take apart the works being examained and probe their inner mechanisms to uncover how and why they have the effects they do.

Critics, therefore, are not listeners or viewers or readers. Critics necessarily distance themselves from the works they examine. The intended audience, the listener, viewer or reader, becomes involved with the work, becomes absorbed by the work. Listeners, viewers and readers, however, often turn to the critics with the question "What does it mean?" Critics, therefore, have taken on the function of interpreting the works they examine. Art critics will tell the viewer what the Mona Lisa means, music critics will tell the listener what Beethoven's Fifth Symphony means, and biblical critics will tell the reader what the parable of the good Samaritan or the Book of Jonah means. Each type of critic uses methods developed for analyzing the inner mechanisms of a work to tell those for whom the work is intended, i.e., the audience, what it means.

Until recently the gap between biblical critics and biblical readers has been progressively widening. Many readers of the Bible have become so awed by the critics that they feel inadequate when faced with the question of what a given text means and must rely on an authoritative critic. Other readers have been angered by the presumed hegemony of the critics and have chosen to ignore them and interpret the texts for themselves according to easy to grasp techniques. Recent critical methodologies, however, are lessening the gap between critic and reader by recognizing the role of the reader in the interpretive process. These new methods are still forms of criticism whose primary function is to examine how and why texts have the effect they do have. What is new and distinctive about these methods is their insistence that any analysis of the inner mechanisms of a text must include the involvement of the reader.

3. THE LIMITATIONS OF CRITICAL METHODOLOGIES

In biblical studies a vast array of critical methods have been developed in modern times: literary source criticism, form criticism, redaction criticism, structuralism, canonical criticism, reader-response criticism, and a variety of others. All of these are attempts to analyze how and why the biblical text does whatever it does—just as music criticism, drama criticism and art criticism are all attempts to explain how and why certain works do what they do.

It is important to recognize that each of the methods used in biblical studies is limited. No method is universal, no method is a panacea. All of the different kinds of criticism are simply different methods that can be used, each of which has its possibilities, each of which can do something. With each of the methods, however, it is important to recognize what it is that it does or does not do, and what the real value of what it does is for the understanding of Scripture. The same considerations apply to any methodology that is productive of benefits, e.g., dentistry. There are all kinds of different methods that dentists use, with many dentists specializing in one area, e.g., orthodontists and dental surgeons. If something is wrong or the need exists, one must go to the right specialist who will utilize the right method. There is no one method that will solve all problems dealing with teeth. Each method has its capabilities and is to be used to accomplish certain things.

Sometimes in biblical studies scholars fail to recognize the limitations of their methodologies. There are some who proceed almost as if one given method could solve everything. What is really dangerous about this approach is not so much that the method will fail but that the scholars using the method will be satisfied with its inadequate results. Another example from the health sciences can illustrate this danger. A few years ago, two substances relating to cancer, saccharin and laetril, were under investigation by government health agencies. Saccharin was thought to be a possible cause of cancer, and some wanted its production and sale banned. Since the evidence was not conclusive, it was decided not to ban saccharin but merely to label products containing it as potential health hazards. Laetril, on the other hand, was being promoted as a cure for cancer. There was no evidence of any harmful effects, but because there was no evidence of any beneficial effects the government decided to ban it. At the time some commentators marveled at the apparent discrepancy: saccharin which might cause cancer was not banned while the harmless substance laetril was banned. Nevertheless, the decisions by these agencies do serve to highlight the seriousness of a false cure. In a similar fashion, great harm can be done by thinking that exegetical methodologies can do what, in fact, they cannot do. It is important in analyzing methods to recognize exactly what each method can do, and then to evaluate it in terms of just how worthwhile that method is.

4. THE NECESSITY OF CRITICAL METHODOLOGIES

Not only is each critical methodology limited in what it can do but, in a certain sense, critical methodologies are not even needed. Critics, whether they are biblical critics, art critics or any other kind of critics, can attempt to tell audiences why they appreciate or fail to appreciate a given work of art. Critics can tell them what the work is trying to do. They can tell them how well or how poorly it does it. In the final analysis, however, critics are not necessary. The thousands of fans attending the Springsteen concert mentioned earlier had no need for a music critic to help them appreciate his music. They appreciated him; I did not. None of us, however, needed a critic to enable us to respond to the music.

An important distinction was drawn a few years ago by George Steiner between syllabus and canon (" 'Critic'/'Reader'," *New Literary History* 10 [1979] 445–47). Critics, using their methodologies, tell audiences what is or is not worth watching or listening to or reading. The verdict of critics often determines which shows remain on Broadway and which close after opening night. What critics prescribe is a syllabus, a listing of what ought to be appreciated. Audiences, on the other hand, produce canons, i.e., listings of what have been appreciated. While critics choose the syllabus, it is more often the case that the canon chooses the audience. Readers, for example, are read by the text as much as they read it. The things one reads that resonate with one's very being are the things that are remembered and repeated, the things that become canonical. Steiner's distinction was intended primarily for contemporary secular literature but it applies equally well to the books of the Bible. The books of the Bible were appreciated by their earliest audiences, i.e., became canonical before the critics placed them on the syllabus. They were read before they were subjected to critical analysis.

One interesting thing that can happen, and often does, is that critics will examine a work and decide that nobody should appreciate it or that it really is not all that great. Then people will proceed to read or watch or listen to that given work and end up liking it. This phenomenon occurred when the movie "The Sound of Music" was first released. Many of the earliest articles by movie critics considered this movie to be rather mediocre but it turned out to be one of the biggest money-makers that Hollywood has ever produced. The critics missed the boat. There was something there that the critics did not see that the movie-going audience did see. The movie-going audience paid not the slightest bit of attention to the critics. They liked it and they went, and they told their friends and their friends went. Earlier critics tried to exclude "The Sound of Music" from the syllabus. Subsequent critics were faced with the task of explaining how it became part of the canon.

What happened with this movie is related to a complaint raised by proponents of some of the new directions in biblical studies, against previous critical methods. The complaint is that biblical scholars have taken the Bible away from the people. Biblical scholars have rather successfully convinced many in the community of believers that only they, the biblical scholars, can really appreciate the Bible. They are the only ones who can determine what it means. The rest of the community must sit up and listen to the biblical scholars explain what the Bible means. Such, in fact, is not the case. Any believing Christian can read the Bible and can appreciate the Bible because the Bible does something to its readers. The role of the critic is primarily to explain how and why and in what way the Bible does what it does. Compared to the role of the readers, the role of critics is entirely secondary.

The biblical authors did not write for critics; they wrote for their readers. The nature of their writing was such that it could be read and understood by readers without the aid of critics or exegetes. Paul wrote to the community at Galatia. His letter to them was read by them and by countless other Christians over the past two thousand years. His letter has also been read and analyzed by biblical critics, but the nature of the letter itself does not require the involvement of critics. Some modern writers do seem to be writing for critics. Knowing that literary critics will analyze their works, they write with a view toward the expected analysis. Some, it seems, even deliberately flaunt the norms of communication agreed upon by critics just to give these critics something to reconsider. This activity, however, is a modern phenomenon. None of the books of the Bible were written with a view toward what later critics would do with them. All of them were written with a view toward what effect they would have on their readers.

5. READER INTERPRETATION

The Bible, like a work of art, affects its readers. As in all art, its affective aspect is of primary importance. That is one of the things the Springsteen article points out. Springsteen's music affects his listeners, and what he is intent upon doing is designing his album and his songs and his sounds and everything else in such a way that they will have an affect on those who listen. The Bible is very much the same. It has a message that it is trying to communicate, but a message it communicates only if it is received. In this respect the Bible and all art forms are very much like sound.

The motion of the prongs of a tuning fork sets up periodic waves in the surrounding air. Each forward movement of a prong compresses the air in front of it, and each backward movement rarefies the air. These conditions are transmitted outward from the fork as a wave disturbance comprising so-called condensations and rarefactions. Upon entering the ear, these waves produce the sensation of sound, and the waves themselves are called sound waves (E. Hausmann and E. Slack, *Physics* [N.Y.: Van Nostrand, 1948], p. 553).

Sound, according to this description, depends on the hearer. If a tree falls down in the woods it normally makes a loud crashing sound. However, what if nobody is there to hear it? Does a tree falling down in the woods, with nobody around, make a sound? The answer is no. It does not make a sound. Sound is something that exists wholly in the human being. Without a human being, or without some kind of an ear, there is no sound. All that happens when a tree crashes in the woods, or when anything happens that is productive of sound, is that air is condensed and rarefied. This condensed and rarefied air then moves out in a wave pattern from the source of the disturbance. It is just like throwing a pebble in a pond and watching the waves, which are condensed and rarefied water, move away from the point where the pebble was thrown in. All that happens when one rings a bell or knocks a tree down in the woods is the generation of waves consisting of condensed and rarefied air. Upon entering the ear this condensed and rarefied air produces a sensation of sound. That is where sound is, in the ear, or in the brain that translates what goes into the ear. Apart from the human ear there is no sound. All there is is condensed and rarefied air.

According to the new developments in biblical criticism to be discussed in the remaining chapters of this book the Bible is very much like sound. Apart from the reader, all that the Scriptures are is something like condensed and rarefied air. The books of the Bible were written to have an effect on the reader. It is the reader who makes meaning out of the biblical text.

6. THE PROMISE OF NEW METHODS

Over the centuries a wide variety of critical methodologies have been used to analyze the Scriptures. All of these have contributed, in some way, to the believing community's appreciation of the role of the Scriptures in its faith and life. These methodologies have been harmful only when it was assumed that their results were of greater significance than was actually the case. If, for example, the full meaning of Scripture were assumed to lie in actual historical events recoverable by the historical-critical method, then the real depth of meaning and inexhaustible richness of the Scriptures would be lost. Even worse, if scholars should conclude, as many have, that very little historical accuracy is actually recoverable, then the Scriptures would become almost meaningless for the faith and life of the community. Few if any scholars have followed this hypothetical scenario but some unfortunate tendencies have arisen among biblical scholars. Previous theories of verbal inspiration have been shattered by the discoveries of source, form and redaction criticism. The resulting tendency among recent scholars has been to emphasize the human activity involved in the production of Scripture while politely ignoring the question of precisely how they are of divine origin.

The practitioners of the new developments to be discussed in this book, structuralism, reader-response criticism and canonical criticism, are all noteworthy for their almost unanimous insistence that their methods do not exhaust the meaning of the biblical texts. Structuralists especially insist that other methods must be used in order to bring out the full meaning. Structurralists themselves are merely uncovering levels of meaning that other methods have not yet sufficiently recognized.

In addition to recognizing their own limitations, the new methodologies being developed hold out the promise of correcting many of the deficiencies of currently used methodologies. Each in its own way places substantial emphasis on the user of the text, i.e., the reader or the community of faith. Each offers new ways of understanding how and why these texts were accepted as pertaining to the sacred literature of the community. Finally, the full implications of reader-response criticism and canonical criticism can yield a new way of expressing the divine inspiration of Scripture, a way that is in harmony with early Christian and medieval understandings of inspiration.

SUGGESTIONS FOR FURTHER READING

Brown, R.E., *The Critical Meaning of the Bible* (New York: Paulist, 1981).

Henry, P., *New Directions in New Testament Study* (Philadelphia: Westminster, 1979).

Poland, L., *Literary Criticism and Biblical Hermeneutics* (Chico: Scholars, 1985).

Reese, J., *Experiencing the Good News: The New Testament as Communication* (Wilmington: Glazier, 1984).

Steiner, G., " 'Critic'/'Reader'," *New Literary History* 10 (1979) 23–52.

Chapter 2

BIBLICAL CRITICISM IN THE HISTORY OF THE CHURCH

Modern biblical criticism developed among liberal Protestant scholars during the nineteenth century. Applying to the Bible techniques derived from profane sciences they began to call into question time honored assumptions about the nature and meaning of the various books of the Bible. Catholics and conservative Protestants strongly opposed these new developments which were seen as undermining the integrity and authority of the Scriptures. In the early part of the twentieth century the Pontifical Biblical Commission and Protestant fundamentalists stood almost shoulder to shoulder in opposing the conclusions of biblical critics.

As the century wore on conservative Protestant scholars began to use, with caution, those techniques of biblical criticism that were seen to serve and not destroy their faith. In 1942, with the publication of the papal encyclical *Divino Afflante Spiritu,* the Catholic Church wholeheartedly embraced current techniques of biblical criticism, encouraging Catholic scholars to utilize these techniques in determining "the literal sense of the biblical texts, that is, the sense the inspired authors intended to give their works." About the same time that this encyclical was published, literary critics in England and America were developing what came to be known as the New Criticism, an approach to literature that insists that the intention of the author ought not to be considered in determining the meaning of a work of literature. The New Criticism will be discussed in greater detail in Chapter V. It is mentioned here only to illustrate the fact that not only does biblical criticism borrow its methodologies from secular studies but it is often decades or even centuries behind these studies. Such has been the case throughout the history of the Christian Church.

1. METHODS DERIVED FROM PROFANE STUDIES

1.1 Alexandria

Long before Christianity came on the scene, Jewish scholars had developed highly refined methods for interpreting their sacred literature. Some of these methods are quite evident in parts of the New Testament where various authors allude to and interpret Old Testament passages. Jewish interpretive techniques continued to be used by Christians for understanding the writings of both the Old and New Testaments but gradually lost ground to methodologies derived from the Graeco-Roman world.

The most important center for the development of these new methodologies was Alexandria, which, during the early Christian centuries, was the intellectual capital of the Graeco-Roman world. What happened at Alexandria is what has continued to happen right up to the present day, i.e., ideas derived from a particular philosophy were used to develop a methodology for examining and interpreting the Scriptures. At Alexandria the philosophical system used was that of Plato. The insight that influenced biblical interpretation was the Platonic theory that the material world, the world of experience, was not the real world but merely a shadow of reality. The real world was the world of forms, or the world of ideas. Applying this theory to the problem of biblical interpretation yielded the method known as allegorical interpretation.

Christians were not the first to use this method. During the first century A.D. Philo of Alexandria, a Jewish philosopher, had developed an allegorical method for interpreting the sacred literature of the Jews. This method was further refined and developed by Christian scholars, reaching its fullest expression in the work of the third century scholar, Origen of Alexandria. According to Origen, biblical texts can be read according to their literal, historical sense, but this sense provides only a shadow of the reality that the Scriptures are intended to communicate. The real world of the biblical texts is the world of faith which can be attained when one recognizes that the literal, historical sense of Scripture symbolizes this real world of faith. Applying Origen's methodology by treating the biblical texts as allegories of the real world of faith, one can ascend to three successive levels of meaning: first, the present reality of Christ and his Church; second, insights pertaining to moral behavior; finally, the heavenly and eschatological realities that are the object of Christian hope. For Origen, not only the New Testament but also the Old Testament can be read allegorically by believing Christians and be understood as representing Christ and his Church, Christian living, and the goal of Christian existence.

1.2 Scholastic Theology

The allegorical method continued as the dominant methodology for biblical interpretation until the thirteenth century when scholastic theologians looked to another pagan philosophical system for insights that shaped their methodologies. The pagan philosophical system was that of Aristotle. The theologian who was most influential in introducing Aristotelian ideas into biblical interpretation was St. Thomas Aquinas who structured his theological system according to the rigorous demands of Aristotelian logic and dialectic. He looked to the Scriptures for clear evidence in support of the truths of faith he was analyzing. Since allegory did not suit the demands of rigorous argumentation, St. Thomas placed supreme importance on the literal sense of Scripture. He did not deny that the Old Testament prefigured the realities of Christ and Christian existence, nor that there were indeed spiritual or mystical senses of passages that went beyond the literal sense. He did maintain, however, that these other senses contained nothing that could not be found elsewhere in Scripture in the literal sense, and that only the literal sense could be used in theological argumentation.

St. Thomas' insistence on the literal sense excluded allegorical interpretation but did not exclude recognizing that the Bible often employs metaphorical or figurative language. When the language used is figurative, then the literal sense is the figurative sense. As a result, the literal sense was much richer than a sense that could be derived simply from a literal reading of the text. So rich was the literal sense for St. Thomas that it could only be discovered when the Scriptures were read in the light of the traditions of the Church.

Scholastic theology left the Christian world with a single-minded concern for the literal, historical sense of Scripture, a concern which remains manifest among most Christians right up to the present day. Scholastic theology had another, less fortunate, consequence. The rigorous methodology developed under the influence of Aristotelian philosophy eventually degenerated into the practice of proof-texting, searching the Scriptures for texts whose literal sense supports or proves doctrines that one accepts independent of their scriptural foundation, a practice which likewise continues to the present day.

1.3 Renaissance Humanism

By the sixteenth century, Scholastic theology had become dry and lifeless. A new wave of scholars appeared on the scene who were more interested in studying the classic literature of the ancient Greeks and Romans than in studying the theological treatises of late Scholasticism. New techniques were developed, arising out of the emerging philosophy of humanism, for literary analysis, techniques that were first applied to classic literature but which were eventually applied to the Bible. The most notable figure for the new direction that biblical scholarship was to take was Erasmus of Rotterdam, an older contemporary of Martin Luther. He had considerable influence on the development of Luther's ideas but, despite appeals from Luther, he steadfastly refused to join the Reformation movement.

Erasmus had embraced the humanist concern for recovering the original meaning of ancient literature. Applying the newly developed methodologies to the Bible, he sought not only to recover the original meaning of the text but, more fundamentally, to recover the original text itself. Centuries of copying the Bible by hand had resulted in the introduction of scribal errors that were many times compounded. By the sixteenth century there were enormous discrepancies among the Bibles then in use. Erasmus' most memorable achievement was his publication of the first critical edition of the Greek New Testament in 1516. This work, called *Novum Instrumentum,* was also the first printed edition of the Greek New Testament. By comparing a number of diverse manuscripts according to humanist principles of literary analysis, Erasmus produced what he felt was a more accurate representation of the original text. His edition was actually far from accurate, but the work he began has continued to the present day in that branch of biblical studies known as text criticism.

In addition to attempting to recover the original text of the New Testament, Erasmus was also involved in the humanist endeavor to recover the original literal meaning of the text. Humanist scholars generally maintained that what Scholastic theologians were assuming to be the literal meaning of the text did not stand the test of critical literary analysis. Though Erasmus' interpretation of Scripture was often at odds with that of theologians and ecclesiastics of his day, he always insisted that the literary analysis of Scripture had to be done in the context of the faith of the Church. Other humanists were not of the same mind and began using their new interpretations of Scripture as a weapon against the Church. Though Erasmus remained loyal to the Catholic Church throughout his life, the Protestant Reformation, with its appeal to the Scriptures as an authority superior to the Church, is actually rooted in the new direction given to biblical studies by Erasmus and other humanists.

1.4 Reformation

Erasmus' understanding of what the Bible was and how it was to be used is fundamentally the same as an understanding to be discussed in Chapters VIII and IX. The Bible, in this understanding, is primarily the Church's book canonized by the Church, given its continuing meaning by the Church. This was the common understanding of Scripture from the earliest centuries. This idea, however, the idea that the Bible is the Church's book, was radically changed by the Reformation. The Bible became the criterion whereby the Church could be judged and criticized. For Wycliffe and Huss, and especially for Luther and Zwingli and their followers, the Bible became a weapon to be used against the Church. Their understanding of the Bible differed radically from the understanding of the Bible as the Church's book, the Bible which is canonized by the Church, taken up into the life of the Church precisely because it is seen as serving the Church. The reformers, in the interest of reform, were actually driving a wedge between the Bible and the Church.

The understanding of the Bible as a document that has meaning and validity apart from the Church soon led to the problem of private interpretation. After the more sober efforts of people like Luther, Calvin and Zwingli, there soon appeared the Anabaptists, the Ranters, the Seekers and the Quakers. All of these groups flourished in the seventeenth century when private interpretation went haywire. It was at this point in time that sober, sensible Protestant scholars and churchmen, Lutherans, Calvinists, and Anglicans, insisted that corrective measures were needed. There was obviously something wrong with the various sectarians doing whatever they wanted to do with the Bible. If the Bible was to be the solid foundation and the criterion of the Church's life and existence, there had to be a clear and secure method for interpreting it.

A division occurred at this time within Protestantism, which continues to the present day, between those willing to use critical methodologies to interpret the Scriptures and those who insist on allowing the text to speak for itself, the reader being guided by the light of the Holy Spirit. Though the boundary lines of this division are not always clear, there have been and still are liberals who are willing to follow the lead of critical scholarship wherever that might lead and conservatives who are suspicious of any new insights that threaten traditional convictions.

It was at this time, among those who were open to critical methodologies, that objective historical criticism, using the methodology of Enlightenment scholarship, came on the scene

and effectively took the Bible out of the Church's lectern and put
it in the scholars' study. This step was not too hard to take either
for the scholars or for the Protestant churchmen because the Bible had already been effectively divorced from the Church. The
Reformation churches desperately needed the Bible for solidity,
for stability, because the Bible was all they had. They had eliminated or significantly curtailed the effectiveness and meaningfulness of the hierarchical, sacramental Church. They had the
Bible, but they needed a Bible that was solid. They, therefore,
put the Bible in the scholars' study and used the methods of Enlightenment scholarship to make of the Bible something that is
solid and objective on which Reformation Christianity could
stand.

Reformed Christianity needed objective, historical biblical
scholarship. Today virtually all Protestants, whether they are liberal or conservative, view the Bible in a way that accords to it an
existence separate from the faith of the community. The believing community is bracketed out in biblical scholarship, whether
it be conservative or liberal Protestant scholarship. Even Catholics who follow the historical-critical method have done basically
the same thing. They have bracketed out the believing community in applying their critical methodology to the study of the Bible.

1.5 Nineteenth Century

The nineteenth century was characterized by the emergence of new philosophical systems, notably Hegelian Dialectic,
and revolutionary developments in the physical sciences. One of
these developments, the theory of evolution, was to have a direct
influence on biblical scholarship. Other developments exerted
an influence that was more indirect but no less profound. The
general success achieved in the physical sciences led scholars in
other fields to seek the same objective certitude that was available in the sciences. Especially in the field of history, scholars
were striving for the kind of objective certitude that would make
their discipline an exact science.

In the early part of the nineteenth century, Ferdinand

Bauer, the leader of the Tübingen school, raised New Testament scholarship to the scientific level. He saw the New Testament as the product of the history of early Christianity, a history which, according to his Hegelian principles, was one of tension, struggle and eventual reconciliation. He was especially concerned with the conflict between Peter, the Jewish legalist, and Paul, the libertine, but he recognized as well a distinction between Jesus, the Jewish preacher, and subsequent developments in Christianity. One of his students, David Strauss, considered the Jesus of the Gospels to be a creation of later Christianity, and he set about the task of recovering the real Jesus, using the historical methodologies of nineteenth century scholarship. He introduced the concept of myth into New Testament analysis as a way of explaining the seemingly historical, but really non-historical, modes of expression used especially by the Gospel writers. At the end of his work he confessed that though the Gospels do give us some historical information about Jesus, the evidence is too fragmentary to write a meaningful life of Jesus.

Strauss considered the task of recovering the historical Jesus to be an impossibility and was satisfied to find the real meaning of the Gospels in the deeper meaning of the myths which the early Christian community created to give expression to their faith. Strauss' work, nevertheless, launched what came to be known as the Quest for the Historical Jesus, a quest pursued by liberal Protestant scholars for the rest of the nineteenth century. Though there was general agreement by the early twentieth century that the quest had failed, it has been taken up again and again by biblical scholars, indicating that the nineteenth century concern for historical objectivity has had a continuing influence on biblical criticism.

The most significant development of the nineteenth century, however, was the use by biblical scholars of the methodology of literary source criticism. Literary scholars had developed highly refined methods for examining a text and determining what sources the author utilized in composing the text. They were even able to propose hypothetical reconstructions of sources which an author must have used but which were no longer available. This methodology was used and adapted by biblical scholars in the light of their general acceptance of Hegelian dialectical philosophy and also their acceptance of the theory of evolution.

For most biblical scholars who employed literary source criticism, the religion of ancient Israel, as well as the religion of the New Testament, evolved from more primitive forms. This evolutionary process can be recaptured as one uncovers and reconstructs the sources that preexisted the books of the Bible. The most notable achievements of this methodology were the four-source theory, which was used to explain the diverse traditions found in the Pentateuch, and the two-source theory, which was used to explain the literary relationships among the Synoptic Gospels.

2. RELATIONSHIP BETWEEN CRITICAL METHODS AND CHURCH AUTHORITIES

Ecclesiastical authorities have always been cautious about importing profane methodologies into the study of the Bible. Only when these methods had proven their worth were they accepted. Origen was condemned in his own lifetime, but his allegorical method eventually became the mainstay of the Church until the rise of Scholasticism. St. Thomas Aquinas was condemned for his use of the methodology of the pagan Aristotle, but his new literal, historical approach eventually supplanted the allegorical approach. In the early part of the twentieth century most ecclesiastical authorities, both Catholic and Protestant, were reluctant to accept the conclusions of the historical-critical method and questioned the appropriateness of using that methodology for the study of Scripture. As it became clear that the results of the historical-critical method supported rather than endangered Christian faith, most of these authorities, including fundamentalists, began to accept the validity of this method.

There is, however, a significant difference between the historical-critical method and most other methods both past and present. Methods that arose in the past had always acknowledged the primacy of the Church in the interpretation of Scripture. Even the Renaissance humanist Erasmus, who was highly critical of the Church because of conclusions derived from his methods, would never claim that his methodological conclusions were of greater authority than the authority of the Church. The historical-critical method is actually the first methodology to win the approval of ecclesiastical authorities while the practitioners of the methodology claim for that methodology an independence from these authorities. Some of the more recent methodologies to be discussed in this book, on the other hand, are moving in the direction of a closer relationship with the organized believing and worshiping Christian community.

One can only speculate about why ecclesiastical authorities seem, at present, to look more favorably upon the historical-critical method than upon these newer methods. One possible reason is that the historical-critical method, by its very nature, does not generate conclusions that challenge the contemporary life situation of Christian communities. Some of the newer methods, with their emphasis on systems of convictions, reader involvement and ecclesial self-understanding, can generate conclusions that are more lively and meaningful but that also might appear to challenge the status quo.

SUGGESTIONS FOR FURTHER READING

Frei, H. W., *The Eclipse of Biblical Narrative: A Study of 18th and 19th Century Hermeneutics* (New Haven: Yale University, 1974).

Froehlich, K., *Biblical Interpretation in the Early Church* (Philadelphia: Fortress, 1985).

Grant, R. M., and D. Tracy, *A Short History of the Interpretation of the Bible* (2nd ed., revised and enlarged; Philadelphia: Fortress, 1984).

Kealy, S. P., *Mark's Gospel: A History of Its Interpretation* (New York: Paulist, 1982).

Reventlow, H. G., *The Authority of the Bible and the Rise of the Modern World* (Philadelphia: Fortress, 1984).

Trigg, J. W., *Origen: The Bible and Philosophy in the Third-Century Church* (Atlanta: John Knox, 1983).

Chapter 3

DIACHRONIC AND SYNCHRONIC
METHODOLOGIES

As explained in Chapter I, there are a wide variety of methods that are used in biblical scholarship. These methods can, for the most part, be classified as either diachronic or synchronic. Literally the term diachronic means through time (Greek prefix *dia*, through), the term synchronic means with time (Greek prefix *syn*, with). Diachronic analysis involves viewing things as having been constituted by or as deriving their meaning from an historical progression, i.e., viewing them through time. Synchronic analysis involves viewing things in and of themselves apart from the historical progression of which they are a part. The chart in figure 3.1 illustrates the various stages in the historical progression that might be considered in a diachronic analysis of a biblical text. The chart in figure 3.2 describes the synchronic approach as an approach which considers what a thing is in and of itself at a given moment in time, or at any moment in time.

1. HISTORICAL-CRITICAL METHOD (DIACHRONIC)

The historical-critical method is an extremely powerful method for analyzing biblical texts. It is essentially diachronic and in recent generations has been the method used almost exclusively by the overwhelming majority of biblical scholars, both Catholic and Protestant. Even fundamentalists have recognized

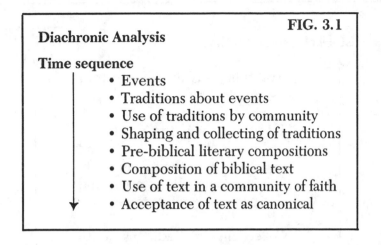

FIG. 3.1

Diachronic Analysis

Time sequence
- Events
- Traditions about events
- Use of traditions by community
- Shaping and collecting of traditions
- Pre-biblical literary compositions
- Composition of biblical text
- Use of text in a community of faith
- Acceptance of text as canonical

the validity and power of this method and have used it to the extent that its results could be harmonized with their religious concerns. This method is a composite method that began developing in the nineteenth century and now embraces various distinct methodologies such as literary source criticism, form criticism and redaction or composition criticism. This composite approach to the Scriptures is what is referred to globally as the historical-critical method. The chart in figure 3.3 describes the various diachronic stages leading up to the composition of Matthew's Gospel which are analyzed by the various methods included in the historical-critical method.

1.1 Literary Source Criticism

The historical-critical method began to develop when, as mentioned in the last chapter, nineteenth century biblical schol-

FIG. 3.2

Synchronic Analysis

Time sequence
- Text itself $\begin{cases} \text{at a given point in time, or} \\ \text{at any point in time} \end{cases}$

Historical-Critical Method

FIG. 3.3

Explanation

Events in Jesus' life referred to or implied by the Gospels

Traditions about the words and deeds of Jesus as shaped and used by the community (e.g., miracle stories and pronouncement stories)

Collections of traditions (e.g., collections of parables underlying Matthew 13, or of sayings in Sermon on the Mount)

Sources used by Matthew (i.e., Mark, Q, and Special Matthean sources)

Text of Matthew's Gospel as composed by the final redactor/author

Analysis

ars applied the method of literary source criticism to the Bible. The first stage of an historical-critical analysis consists of analyzing a text, like Matthew's Gospel, in terms of its sources. Looking at Matthew, Mark and Luke it is obvious that there was some kind of literary dependence, i.e., that someone copied from someone else. The methodology of literary source criticism enables one to determine who copied from whom. The almost but not quite unanimous conclusion is that both Matthew and Luke copied from Mark. It is also generally recognized that Matthew had an additional source, called Q, which was also used by Luke, and other sources as well which were peculiar to Matthew alone. By using the technique of literary source criticism one is able to go behind the text and back through time to what preceded it.

1.2 Form Criticism

One can go even further back in time by using form criticism to break up the pre-existing sources into their component parts, miracle stories, pronouncement stories and other individual units of the oral tradition that were gradually gathered into collections and eventually entered into the sources which were used in the writing of the Gospels.

The study of the individual units of the oral tradition locates one within the activity of the primitive apostolic community. By considering what was going on in the preaching, the teaching, and the liturgical life of the community one can understand why traditions were preserved, shaped and collected the way they were. From this point in time one might even be able to go back to the actual historical events that underlie these traditions. What exactly happened in Jesus' life and ministry? What did he say? What did he do?

Some practitioners of the methodology of form criticism, notably Rudolf Bultmann and his followers, have suggested the impossibility, or at least inadvisability, of determining what really happened in the life of Jesus. What really mattered, for these critics, was the faith of the primitive community and the traditions in which that faith was expressed. Other practitioners of this method, however, especially Joachim Jeremias, felt that the methodology of form criticism could be used to discover the kernel of historical fact on which the believing community built their traditions. Still others, notably a group of scholars who studied under Bultmann but who subsequently came under the influence of the philosophy of the later Heidegger, a group which included Ernst Kasemann, developed a renewed interest in the events of Jesus' life and embarked on what was called the New Quest for the Historical Jesus.

The historical-critical method is diachronic. It analyzes the text by going back through time. Few scholars have been able to halt its momentum at the traditions of the primitive community as Bultmann felt they should. Though the quest has never succeeded, the diachronic nature of the historical-critical method almost compels scholars to pursue it.

1.3 Evolutionary Explanation

Having discovered the historical antecedents of the text, it then becomes possible to explain how the text came to be. There are actually two separate processes that the chart in figure 3.3 seeks to describe, the analytical process and the evolutionary process. One first analyzes the text by going backwards in time and then one explains the results of this analysis by going forward in time. The analysis goes backwards but the explanation goes forward, explaining the process by which the Gospels came to be.

What the historical-critical method, true to its nineteenth century roots, has come up with is basically an evolutionary explanation of the Gospels. One begins with the events in the life of Jesus. After the death and resurrection of Jesus, the primitive Christian community begins its life, a dynamic life that evolves. Part of the evolution, part of the dynamism of the life of the apostolic community, involves preserving traditions about the life and ministry of Jesus, utilizing these traditions in its preaching, teaching, and liturgy, shaping these traditions, gathering them into larger collections and composing the primitive sources that eventually find their place in the biblical texts.

1.4 Redaction/Composition Criticism

At a further stage in the historical-critical method is the work of redaction criticism or composition criticism. These methods consider the work of the individual authors in using their sources in the composition of the individual books of the Bible. The two terms are sometimes used synonymously, though redaction criticism focuses on the editorial activity of the person who pieced together the sources, while composition criticism implies a concern for the creative activity of an author in producing a unified composition. Though these methods are used by historical-critical scholars and are considered to be a part of that method, their emergence began, among some, to raise suspicions about the validity of the presuppositions of the historical-critical method itself. The historical-critical method, as explained in Chapter II, grew out of nineteenth century developments rooted in an evolutionary theory according to which what comes to be can be explained in terms of the developmental processes that lead up to it. Literary source criticism and form criticism fit well in the evolutionary scheme because they locate their explanation of the texts in the developmental processes that preceded them. Redaction criticism and especially composition criticism locate the explanation in the creative genius of a single writer.

Nevertheless, most redaction/composition critics remain bound to the historical-critical method, continue using the methods of literary source and form criticism, and view the activity of the final redactor or author as a stage in the developmental process, albeit the most important stage.

1.5 Canonical Criticism

There is actually a further type of criticism that some see as pertaining to the historical-critical method, one of the most recent forms of criticism to develop, called canonical criticism. This methodology will be considered in much greater detail in Chapter VIII. It is a method that goes beyond the final composition or the final redaction of the Gospels to further points in time when the works are used by the Church and accepted as canonical (see figure 3.1). For the advocates of canonical criticism, these later points in time are far more important than preceding points, but they are still points in time whose significance depends on the historical processes that preceded them.

At some point in time subsequent to the developmental processes which resulted in a given text, the text was accepted as canonical by the Church. This final acceptance did not happen immediately. It usually happened generations later. Canonical criticism, however, maintains that what is most important is not what happened back in the life of Jesus, not what happened in the evolutionary process during which the traditions were shaped and the sources composed, not even what happened in the activity of the final redactor. What is most important is the text which is accepted by the Church as canonical. This canonically accepted text is the starting point of all biblical exegesis. This text is what the Church has taken into its life and what remains with the Church to the present day.

What is significant about canonical criticism is that, in spite of the fact that it comes out of the historical-critical method and is regarded by many of its practitioners as the final element of that method, it is, in a sense, somewhat opposed to the whole rest of the historical-critical method. The reason for this opposition is canonical criticism's concern for the accepted text rather than for what lies behind the text. What is most important is the inspired text as accepted by the Church, not the historical processes that preceded it. In this respect canonical criticism is more synchronic than diachronic.

2. ADVANTAGES OF SYNCHRONIC METHODOLOGIES

Over the past decade, many of those engaged in using more recently developed critical methods have turned to these methods because of the limitations they have seen in the historical-critical method. What many scholars today are maintaining is that the various methods included in the historical-critical method can produce valid results but what they can do is somewhat limited. They can indeed uncover a great deal about the genetic sequence preceding a text but they do not yield a great deal of insight about the text itself. The various synchronic approaches to be considered in subsequent chapters are primarily concerned with enabling the text itself to yield the depth and richness of its meaning.

2.1 Text Itself or History Behind the Text

The limitations of diachronic exegesis can be brought out by an analogy that is often used by practitioners of synchronic methodologies, the analogy which contrasts a window and a mirror. What are the Gospels? Are the Gospels windows through which one can look at the historical processes that preceded them, or are they mirrors in which one can see a self-contained world? The more recent approaches to biblical studies begin by assuming that the Gospels have something to say in and of themselves. If one thinks of the Gospels as windows, one really fails to see the Gospels themselves. One misses what is there in the text and just looks through the text at something that lies on the other side of the text.

Another analogy that is sometimes used is based on the story of Humpty-Dumpty who fell off the wall. All the king's horses and all the king's men couldn't put Humpty together again. What the historical-critical method has done, in a sense, is that it has taken the Gospels and thrown them off the wall like Humpty-Dumpty. It has shattered them into all kinds of pieces. Literary source criticism couldn't put Humpty together again. Form criticism couldn't put Humpty together again. The evolutionary theory on which these methods are based could not account for the creation of a new being. Once these methods had shattered this new being they could not restore it.

Redaction criticism, however, represents a critical phase in the development of the historical-critical method because redaction criticism, for the first time, took the work of the final redactor seriously. Redaction criticism insists that the Gospels are not simply a collection of forms, a collection of primitive units of the tradition, but that the redactor (the final editor) took these things and put them together in a specific way for a specific purpose. The author of Matthew, for example, took the materials available to him and put them together in a specific way and for a specific purpose.

Redaction criticism does try to put Humpty together again. However, if one really examines what goes on in redaction criticism one sees that though redaction critics do attempt to put Humpty together again they actually fail in their effort. What redaction critics basically focus on are the redactional seams, those elements of the Gospels that manifest the activity of the redactor. If one looks at these redactional seams one can gain insight into the peculiar theology of the redactor, the theology of Mark, the theology of Matthew or the theology of Luke. As a result what redaction criticism basically comes up with is not a reconstituted Humpty-Dumpty but the seams from which one can glean the theology of Humpty-Dumpty. What is arrived at is not Humpty-Dumpty but his theology. Composition critics, it is true, are more interested in the overall compositional activity of the author than in the redactional seams, but though they perceive the work as a unified whole their method is likewise geared toward reconstituting the theology of the author rather than appreciating the work itself.

Structuralists and reader-response critics are concerned with Humpty-Dumpty himself, not some diachronic analysis of him, not a theological analysis of him. Redaction and composition critics, even though they focus on the final product, remain bound to the genetic process and focus on the activity of the author as the final stage in the diachronic process. Structuralists and reader-response critics do not. They focus on the final product itself. They insist that the literary character of, for example, the Gospel narratives must be appreciated before one attempts to use these narratives as evidence for something else, e.g., for history or theology.

2.2 Conceptual Signified and Real World Object

In the view of structuralists and reader-response critics, the Gospel narratives, as we have them, are signs. All signs, as illustrated in figure 3.4, are constituted by two realities, a physical signifier and a conceptual signified. The physical signifier is the immediate object of perception, a red traffic light, the scent of smoke, or a sound that can be recognized as a word. Corresponding to the physical signifier is a conceptual signified, some other reality which the object of perception evokes. A red traffic light alerts one to the need to stop. The scent of smoke indicates that something is burning. Words, whether spoken or written, are likewise signs that signify something other than themselves. The word "tree," for example, is a sign. It signifies the real world object known as a tree, an object with which most people are familiar. The word "pegasus," on the other hand, signifies an

FIG. 3.4

Sign $\left\{\begin{array}{l}\text{conceptual signified}\\\quad\text{(that which the perception evokes)}\\\text{physical signifier}\\\quad\text{(immediate object of perception)}\end{array}\right.$

object that is not part of anyone's real world experience. It is nevertheless just as much a sign as is the word "tree" and similarly is constituted by a physical signifier and a conceptual signified.

Whole narratives are like individual words. They too are signs that signify something other than themselves. A narrative itself, a narrative as a whole, is a sign that consists of a physical signifier and a conceptual signified. To appreciate what a narrative means one has to appreciate both the physical signifier and what it is that it signifies. The conceptual signified, however, is not always a real world object. Narratives are not like traffic lights, nor are they like bank videotapes. Most banks use videotapes as part of their security procedures. If anything undesirable happens the videotape provides an exact picture of what took place, e.g., a bank robbery, and can be used to help remedy the situation. As described in figure 3.5, a bank videotape is a sign

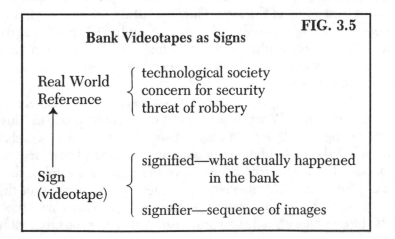

FIG. 3.5

Bank Videotapes as Signs

Real World Reference $\left\{\begin{array}{l}\text{technological society}\\\text{concern for security}\\\text{threat of robbery}\end{array}\right.$

Sign (videotape) $\left\{\begin{array}{l}\text{signified—what actually happened}\\\qquad\qquad\text{in the bank}\\[4pt]\text{signifier—sequence of images}\end{array}\right.$

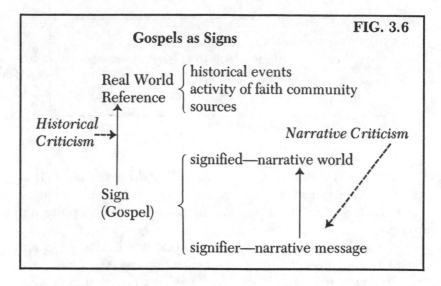

FIG. 3.6

Gospels as Signs

Real World Reference { historical events
activity of faith community
sources

Historical Criticism --->

Narrative Criticism

signified—narrative world

Sign (Gospel) {

signifier—narrative message

whose physical signifier is a sequence of images and whose conceptual signified is a real world object, i.e., what actually happened in a bank on a given day.

While the sign itself symbolizes only what actually happened, one can draw further inferences from the sign about the sociological situation within which the sign functions. The existence of such a sign with such a signification is indicative of an advanced technological society that is concerned about bank security because of the constant threat of robbery. Many other inferences could be drawn but all of these take us beyond the intrinsic meaning of the sign. They constitute the real world reference of the sign but should never be confused with or substituted for the conceptual signified which, in the case of a bank videotape, is itself a real world object, i.e., what actually happened in the bank.

Like bank videotapes, narratives are signs. The Gospel narratives are signs. What historical critics attempt to do, as illustrated in figure 3.6, is to relate the Gospels to the real world that preceded them. In effect they consider as being of primary importance the real world reference of the sign. In so doing they really fail to regard with due seriousness the sign value of the Gospels. Rather than view the Gospels as signs which have their own proper conceptual signified, historical critics too often view the Gospels as windows through which to look at the processes that preceded them.

One might be tempted to suggest that these preceding historical processes are what the Gospels signify. However, even if one considered the Gospel narratives to be signs with real world objects like bank videotapes, what the Gospels would then signify would be the actual events in the life of Jesus but not the various processes connecting the life of Jesus to the Gospel narratives. In point of fact, however, the Gospels—like any narrative—do not signify real world objects. In this respect narratives are more like the word "pegasus" than like the word "tree." Their conceptual signified is not a real world object. The main point of figure 3.6 is to illustrate the fact that although there is a real world object to which the sign, the narrative text, is related, that real world object is not what the sign signifies.

Narratives are signs that have a physical signifier, namely the narrative message, and have as well a conceptual signified which is the narrative world, not the real world. If one views the Gospels synchronically, looks at them in and of themselves, takes them out of a diachronic process, then one can begin to appreciate the sign value of the Gospel narratives.

2.3 Referential Fallacy

The narrative world of the Gospels bears some relationship to the real world, but it is not the real world. By understanding Gospels in terms of their real world reference, biblical critics often commit what is called "the referential fallacy." The referential fallacy consists in assuming that the conceptual signified of a given narrative is the real world and in therefore trying to interpret the elements of that narrative in terms of their reference to the real world. One commits the referential fallacy, for example, when one assumes that the Pharisees of Matthew's Gospel refer to the Pharisees of Jesus' day. One likewise commits the referential fallacy by assuming that the Pharisees of Matthew's Gospel refer to the later Jewish rabbis of Matthew's day.

According to structuralists and reader-response critics the elements of the narrative refer to the narrative world. This narrative world is an artificial creation of the author of the narrative. It is the world in which the story narrated takes place. It usually bears some resemblance to the real world but attempting to understand the narrative in terms of its real world similarities can cause one to miss the whole point of the narrative. The Pharisees of Matthew's Gospel refer to the Pharisees of Matthew's narrative world, a world that needs to be understood and appreciated on its own terms. There is, it is true, a similarity to the real world which will certainly affect the way in which one appreciates the narrative world. The narrative world, however, can only be fully appreciated when one takes the narrative itself seriously, i.e., synchronically.

2.4 Gospel Chronologies

The chronological order of the Gospels provides a good illustration of the above point, for the chronologies in each of the Gospels are different. Each of the Gospels takes various events in the life of Jesus and arranges them in a different chronological order. Various miracles appear in two or more Gospels (the multiplication of the loaves is the only one to appear in all four). Quite frequently, however, the same miracle will appear at a different point in the life of Jesus when it shows up in a second or third Gospel.

The chronology of the final days of Jesus' life is quite confusing especially if one tries to reconcile all four Gospels. John, for example, is quite clear that Jesus died at the same time that the paschal lambs were being sacrificed in the temple. The Synoptics, on the other hand, are quite clear that the Last Supper was a paschal meal in which a sacrificed lamb was consumed and that Jesus died the following day.

> Now before the feast of the Passover . . . during supper . . . (Jn 13:1–2).

> Jesus . . . bowed his head and gave up his spirit. Since it was the day of Preparation . . . (Jn 19:30–31).

On the first day of Unleavened Bread, when they sacrificed
the passover lamb, his disciples said to him, "Where will you
have us go and prepare for you to eat the Passover?" (Mk
14:12; cf. Mt 26:17; Lk 22:7–8).

Numerous diachronic exegetes have attempted to reconstruct the exact chronology of the final days of the life of Jesus
and then to explain how and why the Gospel chronologies appear
as they do. These efforts, however, are rooted in the view that
the real world chronology of the life of Jesus is what is signified
by the Gospel narrative. In fact, the Gospel chronologies signify
the chronologies of the narrative worlds that each of the Gospel
writers has created. There is no reason to expect that they should
correspond to one another and any attempt to reconcile their differences will prove futile. Consider, for example, the following
not quite parallel sequence of events following Jesus' proces-
sional entry into Jerusalem:

Matthew 21	Mark 11
10. he entered Jerusalem	11. he entered Jerusalem
12. entered the temple drove out all who sold and bought	went into the temple
17. went out of the city to Bethany	went out to Bethany
18. in the morning	12. on the following day
19. seeing a fig tree he said to it, "May no fruit ever come from you again!"	13. seeing . . . a fig tree
	14. he said to it, "May no one ever eat fruit from you again!"
	15. entered the temple began to drive out those who sold and . . . bought
	19. when evening came they went out of the city
the fig tree withered at once	20. in the morning they saw the fig tree withered

Historical critics have long recognized that there are different chronologies in the different Gospels. Historical critics, however, have looked at the Gospel narratives as windows opening out to what lies before, opening out all the way back onto the life and ministry of Jesus. They therefore try to figure out what the chronology was in the life of Jesus and how that was transformed according to the various needs of the community and how and why each of the final redactors put it together the way that he did in his Gospel. A synchronic exegete, however, e.g., a structuralist or a reader-response critic, will concentrate on the Gospel itself, on the narrative world that the author has constructed. This narrative world is what is signified and should be the focus of attention.

The main point of all of the above is to emphasize that in order to appreciate what is going on in the Gospels one has to be able to see the narrative sign as signifying this narrative world. The authors of each of the Gospels have, in a sense, painted pictures, have created narrative worlds. By creating these narrative worlds they are doing something to or for their readers. They are bringing about some kind of an effect in their readers by leading them to appreciate the narrative worlds they have constructed.

3. SUMMARY

There are, then, these two radically opposed interpretive methods, diachronic and synchronic. Both are used. Until recently the diachronic method was almost exclusively used. More recently, many scholars are maintaining that the various synchronic methods provide much more fruitful approaches. In analyzing these methods it is important to recognize that each of them is merely a method. It is important, as well, to recognize what each method does, what the method can do for the readers of the Bible. Evaluating the method, one has to consider how worthwhile each method is, i.e., how much each method helps in understanding the text. How much does it help, for example, to be able to figure out the exact words that Jesus spoke? That is something that historical-critical analysis can determine with a degree of probability, but how worthwhile is it to know this kind of information?

Structuralism and reader-response criticism can analyze the Gospels in terms of how they communicate the narrative world of the author of the Gospel. How much does that help? There are many scholars who would suggest that the recently developed synchronic methods provide a great deal more help for appreciating biblical texts than the previously used diachronic methods.

SUGGESTIONS FOR FURTHER READING

Davis, C., "The Theological Career of Historical Criticism of the Bible," *Cross Currents* 32 (1982) 267–284.

Krentz, E., *The Historical-Critical Method* (Philadelphia: Fortress, 1975).

Nations, A. L., "Historical Criticism and the Current Methodological Crisis," *Scottish Journal of Theology* 36 (1983) 59–71.

Patte, D., "The Place of Structural Methods in the Exegetical Task," Chapter 2 of *What Is Structural Exegesis?* (Philadelphia: Fortress, 1976) 1–20.

Petersen, N., "A Literary-Critical Model for Historical Critics," Chapter 2 of *Literary Criticism for New Testament Critics* (Philadelphia: Fortress, 1978) 24–48.

Robinson, J. M., *A New Quest of the Historical Jesus* (Naperville, Ill.: Allenson, 1959).

Stock, A., "The Limits of Historical-Critical Exegesis," *Biblical Theology Bulletin* 13 (1983) 28–31.

Wink, W., *The Bible in Human Transformation: Toward a New Paradigm for Biblical Study* (Philadelphia: Fortress, 1973).

Chapter 4

STRUCTURALISM

Structuralism was the first synchronic exegetical method to have an impact on modern biblical scholarship. At a meeting in France in September 1969 a group of biblical scholars began, for the first time, to apply the insights and methods of structuralism to the biblical texts. Structuralism, a rigorous and elaborate methodology, was itself of rather recent origin and was only beginning to be utilized in other disciplines. Both the newness of the methodology and its rigor have resulted in structuralists being quite explicit in distinguishing the two functions of biblical criticism, i.e., first, explaining how and why the biblical texts have the effect that they do have, and, second, explaining what that effect is, i.e., what the text means. Most of the work of structuralists so far has been devoted to explaining how the texts make sense by analyzing the mechanisms through which a text is meaningful. There have only been a few limited attempts at explaining the meaning of a text by rigorously applying the structuralist methodology.

1. STRUCTURALISM IN GENERAL

Structuralism first appeared in France in the late 1940's. Though some speak of it as a philosophy or as a philosophical system, structuralists themselves would prefer to speak of it as a methodology that can be used for analyzing any human social phenomena. It was first used in the study of anthropology but has since been used in fields as diverse as mathematics and literature. There are, however, certain philosophical presuppositions that virtually all structuralists would agree are essential to the structuralist methodology.

1.1 Presuppositions

Of the presuppositions common to all or most structuralists, those significant for the considerations of this chapter can be reduced to two.

1.1.1 Social Manifestations as Languages

A fundamental presupposition that is basic to all structuralist research is the existence of fixed sets of abstract rules which govern all forms of social activity, whether that activity be language, marriage, science or literature. These fixed rules in all of these diverse areas function in exactly the same way as the rules that define and govern language because, for structuralists, all forms of social activity are forms of communication. Language is simply one of many forms of communication all of which function according to fixed sets of rules.

Most people who communicate with languages are not consciously aware of the phonological and grammatical laws which govern their communication. When they attempt to communicate, however, they succeed in doing so precisely because they adhere to the fixed laws according to which language is structured. Similarly most people who communicate in a variety of other forms of social activity do so without being consciously aware of the fixed set of laws which govern their activity. The work of structuralists to date has been largely the establishment of these fixed sets of laws according to which a variety of forms of social activity take place. As a result their work has typically not been concerned with minute portions of a social manifestation, e.g., a passage from a biblical book or a certain recurring word or idea. Rather their work has been primarily concerned with the complex network of relationships that link and unite all of the different elements of a social manifestation, e.g., an entire biblical book or a complete, well-defined unit within a book such as a parable or a discourse.

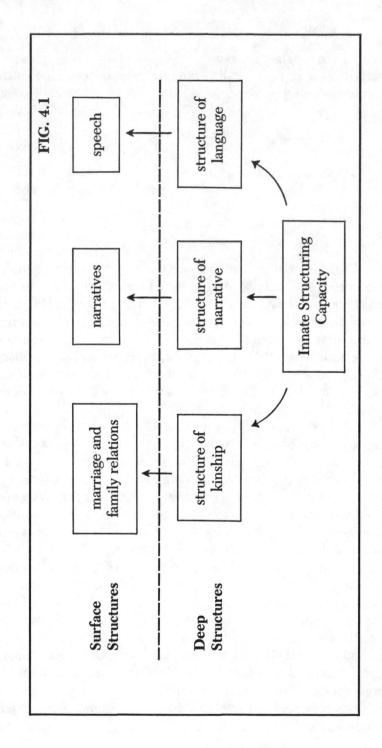

FIG. 4.1

Surface Structures

Deep Structures

speech

narratives

marriage and family relations

structure of language

structure of narrative

structure of kinship

Innate Structuring Capacity

1.1.2 Innate Structuring Capacity

A second presupposition of structuralists, which is really more basic than the first, is that human beings as such have an innate, genetically transmitted and determined mechanism that acts as a structuring force. What is involved in this presupposition is described in figure 4.1. The innate structuring capacity actually limits the possible range of ways of structuring social manifestations or forms of communication. For example, the structure of languages that actually exist represent only a very small part of the spectrum of what is theoretically possible. In a similar fashion, the actual structures of other social manifestations are similarly restricted, for it is the innate structuring capacity of humans that generates the specialized structure for each particular type of activity.

Just as all languages share certain fundamental structural elements, so too do all narratives share certain fundamental structural elements. It is for this reason that structuralists find in narrative units in the Bible, e.g., the parable of the good Samaritan, the same fundamental structure as is found in Russian folk tales.

1.2 Surface and Deep Structures

Figure 4.1 represents the way structuralists view the totality of human social phenomena according to the two presuppositions just explained. There is tremendous diversity which can be observed in human social phenomena, but this diversity occurs only on the surface. There are a wide variety of languages but deep beneath the surface the same basic structure governs all languages. Humans have produced a wide variety of narrative discourses but deep beneath the surface one and the same narrative structure governs all such discourses. Human societies have generated a variety of patterns of marriage and family relations but deep beneath the surface the basic structure of kinship is the same for all.

Structuralism, therefore, is rooted in the belief in the existence of deep structures, for the most part not consciously recognized, that underlie all social manifestations, whether these manifestations pertain to the physical sciences, to the social sciences or to literature. Furthermore, these deep structures have a uniformity that transcends time and space. Because they are derived from an innate structuring capacity they are the same for all peoples of all times and places. The same deep structures underlie the sociological manifestations of primitive Australia and modern Europe. The same deep structures underlie the narrative manifestations of modern America and the Ancient Near East.

1.3 Sound Analogy

In Chapter I it was pointed out that sound does not exist outside of a hearer. All that really exists outside of a hearer is rarefied and condensed air, i.e., sound waves. To call these waves "sound waves" is, however, already to have interpreted them. Apart from the sense of hearing they are merely airwaves, ripples in the air like the ripples that result from throwing a pebble in the water. It is the ear, nervous system and brain that create the sensation of sound. Apart from the ear there is no sound. However, when different people hear sounds they hear the same thing or almost the same thing. All that a speaker immediately accomplishes with the lungs and vocal cords is the sending forth of rarefied and condensed sections of air, i.e., airwaves. These airwaves come to the ears of listeners and they hear sounds. Though all of the listeners create their own sensations of sound the speaker fully expects that each will hear the same sounds. Why? Because the listeners all have ears, and nervous systems, and brains that operate the same way.

The structuralist methodology would suggest that all human experience is analogous to the above explanation of hearing. There are certain deep structures underlying human experience and human communication which function in somewhat the same way that the ears, nervous system and brain function in making sound out of airwaves. A wide variety of readers can all read a given literary work and receive from it roughly the same message or emotive effect because the deep structures that make this work of literature meaningful are part of each person's subconscious or preconscious. The same deep structures are operative in all human beings. It is precisely these deep structures which structuralism seeks to uncover.

2. STRUCTURALIST ANALYSIS OF LITERATURE

The structuralist methodology further maintains that authors do not produce the meaning of their texts. What they do is utilize, unconsciously, the deep structures that make communication possible. Again it is similar to the situation with sound. The activity of a speaker is productive of intelligible sound precisely because there is in each listener the identical capacity to create the sensation of sound out of airwaves. Most people who speak and hear are not the least bit aware of the physical and physiological principles involved in their activity. In a similar way most people who write are not the least bit aware of these deep structures that make their writings meaningful, any more than the people who receive them are aware of these deep structures. These deep structures, nevertheless, are operative both in the work of the writer and in the work of the reader, just as the peculiar operations of ear, nerves and brain, though scarcely ever thought about by either speaker or hearer, are always present and make vocal communication both meaningful and possible.

2.1 Meaning Apart from Author's Intention

One of the complaints often raised against structuralism is that structuralists tend to strip the author of creativity. Structuralists are constantly looking for meaning in deep structures that exist apart from the author's intentionalities. The validity of this approach, however, can be appreciated by considering an Australian boomerang, a device which, if thrown correctly, will zoom out, curve around and come right back to the thrower. It looks like a very simple device, just a bent piece of wood. In fact it is quite complex. It has two arms, and the arms are very different. If one were to try to balance it right in the middle, it would not balance. It tilts because one of the arms is longer and heavier than the other. Brochures that accompany these devices usually describe the nature and function of the arms. The longer and heavier arm is called the dingle arm; the other arm is called the lifting arm. Quite frequently these brochures will contain the rather bizarre assertion that the lifting arm is shaped like the wing of an airplane. What is bizarre about this assertion is that it is anachronistic. It is anachronistic because the Australian aborigines were making boomerangs long before the Wright brothers flew their Kitty Hawk.

It is true, however, that the shape of the lifting arm is essentially the same as the shape of the wing of an airplane. This similarity of shape is by no means a freak coincidence, for the principles of aerodynamics preexisted both the airplane and the boomerang. If the movement of the boomerang were subjected to aerodynamic analysis it would be seen that the lifting arm of the boomerang functions according to the exact same aerodynamic principles as the wing of an airplane. That is why it has the same shape. The aborigines, however, who centuries ago first developed the boomerang, had no knowledge of airplanes, they had no knowledge of aerodynamics, they had no knowledge of anything of this sort. They simply made the boomerang. The aerodynamic principles were there and still are. They exist whether or not anyone is conscious of them.

The fundamental premise of structuralism is essentially the same. There are certain deep structures that underlie all communication. These structures are simply there. Everybody who communicates uses them. Communication is only possible because these structures are there and people use them. Where structuralism finds itself at odds with other forms of interpretation is in the structuralist assertion that at least part of the meaning effect of a literary work is to be found in the deep structures that lie outside the intention of the author.

2.2 Constraints on the Meaning Effect

A characteristic of structuralists in all fields is their tendency not to speak of the meaning of a given social manifestation, e.g., the meaning of a poem or the meaning of a parable. Rather they speak of its meaning effect, a composite effect that results from various levels of meaning that can be discerned in the poem, parable or any other social manifestation.

One can appreciate what is involved in the structuralist concept of meaning effect by comparing texts to hand-woven blankets. Each hand-woven blanket is produced by a specific individual using a loom and using a set of colored threads. Hand-woven blankets, like all works of art, have meaning effects, effects produced on whoever looks at the blanket. The design on the blanket is what brings about the meaning effect. However, the design that is produced and which brings about the meaning effect of the blanket is limited or constrained by the loom and the threads. The designer of the blanket can only operate according to the things that are available. Even more, given the same loom and the same set of threads, an Indian and a Persian would produce two very different hand-woven blankets. It would be possible for someone knowledgeable in these matters to look at these two hypothetical hand-woven blankets and say that one was made by a Persian and that one was made by an Indian. Each has a distinctive appearance. Why? Because there are cultural constraints that are operative, a second level of constraints beyond the constraints of the materials and the tools. There is also a third level of constraints, those arising from the specific characteristics, abilities and limitations of the individual creators, the individuals who actually produce the blankets. Figure 4.2 describes these three levels of constraints that enter into the production of the total meaning effect of a hand-woven blanket.

Using this analogy and applying it to Gospel narratives, structuralists would talk about three levels of structure. Figure 4.3 illustrates the three levels of constraints or the three types of structures that enter into the meaning effect of a Gospel narrative. First of all there are the structures of the enunciation, i.e., the constraints imposed by the author himself and the particular life situation in which and out of which the writing takes place. These structures of the enunciation have, to a large extent, already been studied by practitioners of the historical-critical method. What is involved in these structures is precisely what

```
                                                              FIG. 4.2
                           ⎧ concrete situations and
                  weaver  ⎨
                           ⎩ objectives of weaver

  Structures
  Pertaining                               ⎧ characteristics of a partic-
  to                weaver's culture ⎨ ular culture, e.g., Indian
                                            ⎩ or Persian

                                            ⎧ loom
                  weaving as such ⎨
                                            ⎩ set of threads
```

historical critics mean by the intention of the author, i.e., what the author, using the tools at his disposal, consciously intended to communicate. Structuralists recognize the existence of this level of structures but choose not to consider it not only because it has already been adequately treated by historical critics but also because there is a great deal more in the total meaning effect that remains to be considered. As a result, the structures of the enunciation are generally bracketed out in structuralist analysis.

At a deeper level there are what are called the cultural codes or the cultural structures. These are constraints that are proper to a given people at a given time and place in history. These constraints underlie the activity and the specific life situation of the individual writer. These are constraints of which both the author and the community which is written for are generally consciously

```
                                                              FIG. 4.3
  Structures of        │ Author ⎧ concrete life situation
  the Enunciation   │          ⎨ purpose in composing parable

                                         ⎧ cultural significance
  Cultural            │ Author's culture ⎨ of priest, levite,
  Structures        │                      ⎨ Samaritan, road to
                                         ⎩ Jericho

  Deep                │                    ⎧ narrative structures
  Structures       │ Narrative as such ⎨ mythical structures
```

aware and which likewise have been studied by traditional exegetical methods. These cultural structures operate in the activity and thought processes of both the writer and the community and they have a real effect on the literary product. They therefore have a real place in understanding the meaning effect of a literary product. Significant, for example, for the study of New Testament texts is the culture of first century Palestine. The full meaning effect of the good Samaritan parable involves the nature and role of characters like priests, levites and Samaritans in first century Palestine. Scholars who use the historical-critical method have made substantial use of their knowledge of these cultures in explaining how and why the various New Testament writers wrote as they did.

Finally, there are what the structuralists call the deep structures, analogous to the loom and the set of threads used in the production of blankets. These items are fixed and determined for anyone who weaves a hand-woven blanket. Similarly with regard to any literary compositions there are fixed structures that are proper not merely to a given people at a given time and place in history but that are proper to human beings as such. There are fixed and determined deep structures that are used by anyone composing a Gospel narrative, i.e., narrative structures and mythical structures, structures which will be explained in greater detail later in this chapter. These structures are there, they preexist and are operative in the work of composition whether one is conscious of them or not. These deep structures are like the principles of aerodynamics that were there when the first boomerang was designed whether or not anyone was aware of them. Like the structures of the enunciation and the cultural structures, these deep structures also enter into the composite meaning effect of the literary work.

Where traditional historical critics are intent on discovering what the author intended to communicate, i.e., the one basic meaning of the text, structuralists acknowledge a plurality of structural meanings. Each of the many different structures of the text carries a level of meaning. The author may have only consciously intended the meaning that historical critics discover as the intention of the author, but the author, as a human being and a member of a given social culture, would have passively assim-

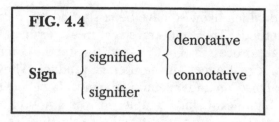

ilated a variety of structures capable of bearing meanings. These structures would have been utilized in the composition of the text and the meanings they bear would be just as much a part of the total meaning effect as the meaning consciously intended by the author. In fact, the meanings that flow from deep structures can be analyzed with even greater certainty than the meaning intended by the author since the identical deep structures are found in all humans and all literary works. Structuralists fully expect that anyone applying their rigorous methodology will arrive at the same conclusions regarding the meaning effects generated by deep structures.

2.3 Literary Works as Signs

The chart in figure 4.4 is an expansion of the chart in figure 3.4 in the previous chapter. A Gospel narrative or any narrative is a sign which involves both a physical signifier and a conceptual signified. The conceptual signified can be further divided into its denotative aspect, that which it directly and literally means, and its connotative aspect, that which it means indirectly or by implication. Some scholars use the term sign only for those things with a direct, denotative signification and use the term symbol to refer to those things with an indirect, connotative signification. In fact, however, all signs have both aspects, though in some, e.g., a traffic light or an operator's manual, the denotative aspect predominates, while in others, e.g., a crucifix or a poem, the connotative aspect predominates.

Literary works are signs with both a denotative meaning and a connotative or symbolic meaning. The intention of the author always involves the denotative meaning of the text and often involves some of the connotative meaning. Structuralism studies

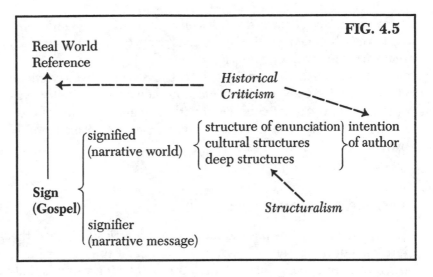

FIG. 4.5

aspects of the connotative meaning of the text that lie beyond the intention of the author. Figure 4.5 is an expansion of figure 3.6 in Chapter III and illustrates the levels of meaning accessible to those using the historical-critical method and the level of meaning studied by structuralists. As mentioned in the last chapter, historical critics are usually not content to uncover the surface meaning of a text but instead go beyond the text, frequently committing the so called referential fallacy, and analyze the real world situation that lies beyond the text. Nevertheless, in the opinion of structuralists, historical critics have adequately studied the meanings of the text that flow from the structure of the enunciation and from the cultural structures.

Structuralists, unlike historical critics, are not tempted to go outside the text to find its real reference, its real meaning. For structuralists the most powerful meaning of a text is that connotative meaning that is carried by the deep structures. The real power of a text is to be found in the system of convictions that precedes the conscious intentions of the author. Precisely because the author holds these convictions it is possible to compose a text with a conscious denotation and connotation that will have a powerful effect on readers. By system of convictions structuralists do not mean a formulated system of ideas, doctrines or ethical values but rather a set of deep convictions that are by their nature unformulatable and can be communicated only indirectly or symbolically. This system of convictions (the semantic universe) can be uncovered only by analyzing the deep structures that carry this symbolic meaning.

Structuralists acknowledge that systems of convictions change as time goes on. Their method, however, is strictly synchronic. They are not concerned with changing systems of convictions but only with the text itself as a static description of its own system of convictions.

3. GOAL OF STRUCTURALISM

Structuralists, as mentioned earlier, practically ignore the intention of the author. They do not deny that the author has a definite intentionality or that the author is trying to say something, but they look instead at the deep structures which, up until the advent of structuralism, had simply been ignored. Historical critics look at the intention of the author or the intention of the believing community. If one looks at a work synchronically one sees that beneath the surface of a literary text there are deep structures that give meaning to the text apart from, or prior to, the intention of the author.

By digging through various structural levels, much as an archeologist digs through levels of occupation, structuralists attempt to arrive at what is called the semantic universe, that world of meaning or system of convictions presupposed by the text. The chart in figure 4.6 describes the process by which structuralists move toward this goal, a process which will be illustrated by specific examples later in this chapter.

Reading this chart from the top down one traces the steps through which structuralists move in searching for deep structures. Structuralists begin at level I, the top level, a narrative manifestation, one complex narrative which is itself a network of elementary narratives. Each one of the four Gospels is an example of a narrative manifestation. At level II one comes to the various elementary narratives that comprise the complex narrative. The examples to be considered later in this chapter are two such elementary narratives, the good Samaritan parable of Luke's Gospel and the passion narrative in Mark. Level III goes

FIG. 4.6

Syntactic Analysis

  I. Narrative manifestation
       a complex narrative as a network of
       elementary narratives, e.g., a Gospel

  II. Elementary narrative
       e.g., a passion narrative, a parable
       or an infancy story

  III. System of narrative programs
       an elementary narrative analyzed in
       terms of the universal narrative
       structure

  IV. System of pertinent transformations
       analysis of those narrative programs
       which have symbolic value

Semantic Analysis

  V. Symbolic or mythical system
       symbolic elements analyzed in terms
       of the universal mythical structure

  VI. Semantic universe
       the system of convictions that are
       presupposed in the narrative
       manifestation

beyond the conscious intention of the author to a deep structure that is operative in all narratives, the system of narrative programs. All narratives consist of highly structured systems of narrative programs, each program being a sequence in which a subject transmits an object to a receiver. Understanding how the parable of the good Samaritan functions, how it communicates, requires uncovering the narrative system that underlies it. Several of the narrative programs from the good Samaritan parable and also from Mark's passion narrative will be detailed later in this chapter.

Once the system of narrative programs is established, one can then move to level IV, the system of pertinent transformations. Each narrative program involves or suggests some kind of a transformation, some kind of change brought about by the subject transmitting an object to a receiver. All of these are important for the denotative meaning of the text, but only some of them are significant for the deeper connotative meaning of the text. The rigorous structuralist methodology enables one to determine which of the transformations are significant and therefore have a deeper symbolic value.

While considering the pertinent transformations one is still operating on the level of the narrative itself, but the specific transformations that take place have symbolic values beyond the surface of the narrative. It is at this point that one moves, in structuralist terms, from syntactic analysis, the analysis of the way in which a text is organized, to semantic analysis, the analysis of the way in which a text has symbolic meaning. Once the symbolic values of the narrative transformations are uncovered one can then move down to level V, to the mythical system. The mythical system that is uncovered will have a structure that is common to all mythical systems, but the specific symbols that are part of this mythical system will point to level VI, the semantic universe. The semantic universe is that rock bottom deep reality, that deep system of convictions, that underlies the work of the author. It is by getting down to this rock bottom universe that structuralists claim they can uncover a dimension of the meaning effect of the text that traditional exegesis has thus far ignored.

Structuralism is uniquely suited for the rigorous study of the symbolic content of a text but, as even its practitioners admit, it cannot do anything else. After a complete structural analysis one will know no more than before about the surface logic that unfolds in a Gospel story or a Pauline letter. One will, however, know a great deal more about the symbolic dimension of the meaning of the text, the system of convictions presupposed (often unconsciously) by the author of the text.

The goal of structuralism is to be able to determine how a given literary work is meaningful and then to use that understanding and go beyond it to the deep system of convictions that underlies it. The possibility of structuralism achieving this goal depends on two things. It depends, first of all, on the legitimacy of its presuppositions, i.e., the existence of deep structures that are common to all humans and to all literary manifestations. It depends, secondly, on the ability of structuralists to discover these structures.

The position of structuralists is much like that of the physical scientist who presupposes that there are uniform laws governing natural phenomena and then sets about to discover these laws, e.g., the laws of aerodynamics or the laws of heredity. Physical scientists operate on the basis of trial and error. When they think they have correctly formulated a law they test it in a controlled experiment. If the experiment does not yield the expected result, then the law must be refined, reformulated and retested. In a similar fashion structuralists have subjected their theories about deep structures to experimentation. Their theoretical formulations have been repeatedly revised and refined to the point where there is now general agreement on the main lines of narrative and mythical structures to be presented in the next section.

4. STRUCTURAL METHODOLOGY

Deep structures function like filters which select those elements in a literary work that can manifest the deep system of convictions that underlies the text. Figure 4.7, a modification of a section of figure 4.5, illustrates the various levels of structures described in figure 4.6 and studied by structuralists. The surface structures of a particular work are those structures peculiar to this work which carry the meaning of the text intended by the author. These structures are studied in order to uncover the narrative system (syntactics) and eventually the symbolic or mythical system (semantics) that underlie the surface structure. These deep structures are common to all literature and to all humans. It is these deep structures that enable certain features that appear in the surface structure to have deep symbolic value. By studying the filtering effect of the deep structures structuralists are able to arrive at the particular semantic universe, the particular system of deep convictions, that underlies a given literary work.

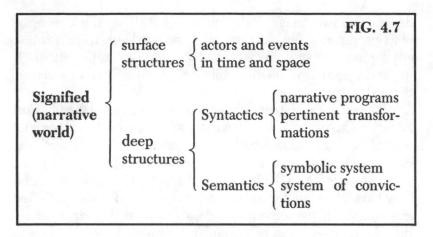

FIG. 4.7

Signified (narrative world)

surface structures { actors and events in time and space

deep structures

Syntactics { narrative programs / pertinent transformations

Semantics { symbolic system / system of convictions

4.1 Narrative Structures

A fundamental premise of structuralism is that every narrative follows basically the same structure. If one does not follow this structure one simply does not have a narrative. Any human being telling a story tells it according to this fixed structure. Every narrative, as illustrated in figure 4.8, consists of three types of sequences or narrative programs. In each of these sequences a subject communicates or transfers an object to a receiver. What each of these elements is and how each functions in bringing about the overall meaning effect of the narrative will be explained in the examples that follow.

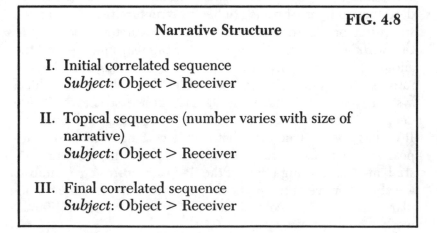

FIG. 4.8

Narrative Structure

I. Initial correlated sequence
   Subject: Object > Receiver

II. Topical sequences (number varies with size of narrative)
    Subject: Object > Receiver

III. Final correlated sequence
    Subject: Object > Receiver

The three types of sequences in any narrative are the initial correlated sequence, the various topical sequences and the final correlated sequence. What these kinds of sequences are can be illustrated with a type of narrative extensively studied by structuralists, i.e., the Russian folk tale. This type of narrative has become quite important in structuralist studies since it has been discovered that the basic structures that are very clear and evident in simple Russian folk tales are the same structures that are found in any narrative.

Every Russian folk tale begins with an initial correlated sequence where the social order is somehow disrupted. In a village or a hamlet the social order is disrupted in a way that the social contract, the acceptable course of human relationships and activities, cannot be carried out. The rest of the narrative consists in attempts to reestablish the social order in such a way that the contract can be carried out. Usually there is an initial subsequence explaining how the social order is disrupted by some kind of villainy. The final correlated sequence shows the social order eventually being reestablished, and then life continuing as normal. Between the initial and final sequences there is a whole series of topical sequences that show how various heroes are mandated to reestablish the social order. When a specific hero actually carries out his mandate to reestablish the social order, the final correlated sequence follows in which the order is reestablished and life goes on as normal.

The structure found in the Russian folk tale is basically the same structure that is found in any narrative. A biblical narrative that has been thoroughly analyzed by structuralists is the parable of the good Samaritan.

> A man was going down from Jerusalem to Jericho, and he fell among robbers, who stripped him and beat him, and departed, leaving him half dead. Now by chance a priest was going down that road; and when he saw him he passed by on the other side. So likewise a levite, when he came to the place and saw him, passed by on the other side. But a Samaritan, as he journeyed, came to where he was; and when he saw him, he had compassion, and went to him and bound up his wounds, pouring on oil and wine; and then set him on his own beast and brought him to an inn, and took care of

him. And the next day he took out two denarii and gave them to the innkeeper, saying, "Take care of him; and whatever more you spend, I will repay you when I come back" (Lk 10:30–35).

In this parable the order that is set up at the beginning, a man going from Jerusalem to Jericho, is disrupted by the activity of the robbers. Various heroes are mandated to reestablish the order, the priest, the levite, and finally the Samaritan who actually accepts his mandate to reestablish the order. The story ends at this point but one can infer that the final correlated sequence will follow, i.e., the man will get to Jericho. The overall structure is, then, the same as that found in the Russian folk tale.

One can look at any other story in the Gospels and discover basically the same structure, e.g., the story of the birth of Jesus in Matthew 1:18–25. There Joseph is about to take Mary as his wife but the order is disrupted when Mary becomes pregnant by the power of the Holy Spirit. Following the basic narrative structure one arrives at the end of the story where the order has been reestablished and Joseph takes Mary as his wife. In the very next story, the story of the magi, their journey to visit Jesus is initially interrupted but eventually the order established at the beginning is brought to completion. Each of these is a simple, straightforward narrative in which the basic narrative structure is easily discerned.

The Gospels as wholes are also narratives, though much more complex. Nevertheless, they too, as true narratives, adhere to the fixed structure for narrative discourse. In each of the Gospels there is an order that has been disrupted, i.e., the order that God desires for his creation, the kingdom of God. In each of the Gospels Jesus is the hero who is mandated to reestablish this order. In each of the Gospels there is a variety of sequences which move toward the eventual success of Jesus' mission. As in the parable of the good Samaritan, the final success of Jesus' mission is not directly affirmed, but left to the reader to infer.

In a simple narrative there would be a limited number of sequences or narrative programs while in a complex narrative

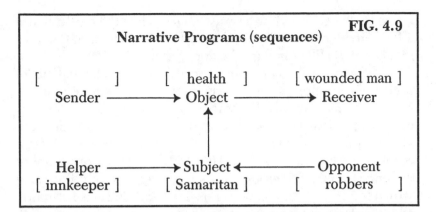

FIG. 4.9

Narrative Programs (sequences)

[   ]   [health]   [wounded man]
    Sender ————————→ Object ————————→ Receiver

    Helper ————————→ Subject ◄———————— Opponent
[innkeeper]   [Samaritan]   [robbers   ]

there would be an enormous number of them. All of them, however, would fit into the basic overall structure of narrative that is common to all narratives. Furthermore, regardless of how many or how few narrative programs or sequences there are, each one of the programs has the same internal structure. Each of the narrative programs can be analyzed in terms of what structuralists call the actantial model, a model which, as described in the chart in figure 4.9 consists of up to six actants. Actants are not to be confused with actors or characters. Actants are roles. The same person, the same character in a narrative, can fulfill the role of different actants in different sequences.

In any given sequence, as mentioned earlier, there is a subject, an object and a receiver. There is also a frequently unnamed but implied sender. Someone, the sender, sends an object to a receiver, as illustrated in the top line of the chart, the communication axis. This communication is facilitated on the volition axis, the vertical line on the chart, by the subject. In the parable of the good Samaritan, someone (sender) wants health (object) to be restored to the wounded man (receiver). The Samaritan (subject) is commissioned or mandated to restore health to the wounded man, as were previously the priest and the levite.

There is also, finally, the power axis, the bottom horizontal line on the chart where the subject is aided by someone or something (the helper) and is hindered by someone or something (the opponent). In the parable of the good Samaritan, the Samaritan is helped by his donkey, his money and the innkeeper. He is hindered by the robbers and the effects of their actions. Any narrative can be analyzed by a series of charts like the one in figure 4.9 where all of the different slots, for each of the narrative programs, can be filled in with the appropriate actants.

The narrative structure of figure 4.8 and the actantial model of figure 4.9 represent deep structures that are operative in all narratives. They are like the aerodynamic principles on the basis of which airplanes or boomerangs fly. They are there, they are given. By digging down one can uncover these structures. If one considers "Matt Houston" or "Hart to Hart" or any of a number of contemporary television shows one sees basically the same structure. All of these shows begin with some kind of a disruption which is followed by various topical sequences where certain people are mandated to do whatever they can to restore the intended order. Eventually the appropriate hero accepts the mandate and at the end of the show the order is restored. Where this structure is intact and operative one has a true narrative.

4.2 Symbolic or Mythical Structures

So far narrative structures have been considered, but there is an even deeper type of structure, i.e., mythical structure, which is found behind and beneath narrative structures. Narratives are sequential, something happens, and then another thing happens and then a third thing happens. One can establish a sequential order in analyzing a narrative. Myths, on the other hand, are paradigmatic. Although myths usually involve narrative elements and often appear to be narratives, what is essential about myths is not the logical sequence of events but rather the pattern or paradigm according to which elements of the myth with symbolic value are ordered and related. A pure myth is a fanciful, fantastic story without a conscious, logical argument but abounding in symbols. The parable of the good Samaritan is not a myth, though it does contain mythical elements. This parable does have a conscious logical argument. It is a true narrative. There are actually very few, if any, pure myths in the Bible. However, just as myths are frequently structured like narratives and can be analyzed according to the narrative structures that are operative within them, so also narratives can be analyzed ac-

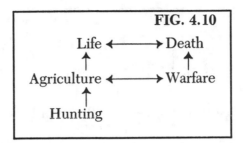

FIG. 4.10

Life ⟷ Death

Agriculture ⟷ Warfare

Hunting

cording to the mythical structures that are operative within them even though they are not, strictly speaking, myths. Quite frequently in biblical narratives one can find mythical structures.

What a myth basically does is resolve oppositions. A myth is a way of coping with the fundamental oppositions that one constantly faces in the course of human living. The elements of the myth, in a pure myth, are simply arranged in some kind of meaningless story. The meaning of the myth is to be found entirely in the manner in which the oppositions, the fundamental oppositions, are overcome, fundamental oppositions like life and death, or heaven and earth, or God and man. These are fundamental oppositions that are so radically opposed that there is no middle ground, there is no way logical minds can bring the two together. Myths overcome these oppositions by providing corresponding oppositions, parallel oppositions, that can be overcome, that do admit of mediation. There is no mediation between life and death. Something or someone is either alive or dead. The way a typical myth would overcome this opposition between life and death would be to replace it with another, parallel opposition that does admit of mediation, e.g., the opposition between agriculture and warfare.

The chart in figure 4.10 sketches out the paradigmatic arrangement of the mythemes, i.e., the fundamental mythical elements, of a myth intended to overcome the opposition between life and death. The mythical story in which these elements might be embedded would have a sequential order but it would be of little consequence. The entire meaning of the myth would be derived from the paradigmatic order of opposed mythemes indicated in the chart.

Agriculture supports life since it involves gathering food

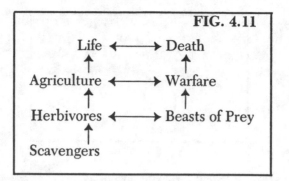

while warfare brings death since it involves killing enemies. Agriculture and warfare are opposed as are life and death, yet they are not so radically opposed that they do not admit of meditation. The mytheme agriculture and the mytheme warfare can be mediated in the mytheme hunting, which like warfare involves killing, but like agriculture involves providing food. Hence, the primary opposition, life and death, which cannot be mediated, is mediated in a myth by the mediation that hunting provides between agriculture and warfare.

The analysis of this mythical structure involves, first of all, recognizing the proportionality that exists between the various pairs of opposition, e.g., life is to death as agriculture is to warfare. Frequently in a myth there will be successive pairs of oppositions, successive proportions. Life and death cannot be mediated. Agriculture and warfare can be mediated by hunting but the distance between agriculture and hunting or between hunting and warfare is still very great. The chart in figure 4.11 illustrates a third pair of oppositions that will be even easier to mediate, herbivorous animals and beasts of prey. Agriculture is to warfare as herbivorous animals are to beasts of prey. The opposition between herbivorous animals and beasts of prey can be mediated by scavengers. A herbivorous animal gathers its vegetarian food. A beast of prey kills other animals for food. Scavengers do not kill, but they eat dead animals that they find.

A typical myth would consist in paradigmatic elements or mythemes, like the above. A story, a very fanciful story, that has no real logical sequence and no real meaning in and of itself, would incorporate various of these elements, but usually not the fundamental elements that are being mediated. One usually has to infer the fundamental mediation brought about by the myth by the significance of the various other elements.

Many biblical narratives, while not being true myths, do contain mythical elements. What structuralists do is examine the pertinent transformations of the narrative structure in order to uncover those significant narrative elements that have symbolic value. Having uncovered these significant narrative elements they can proceed to the corresponding mythical elements in the deeper mythical structure that underlies the narrative and arrange them in their paradigmatic order.

5. GOOD SAMARITAN PARABLE

This kind of mythical analysis can be applied to the parable of the good Samaritan. The overall narrative structure of this parable discussed above is a structure that involves a series of narrative programs in each of which a subject communicates an object to a receiver. Some of these programs involved transformations for which there were opposing transformations in the story. These narrative transformations are the pertinent transformations indicative of oppositions that pertain to the mythical structure. The subjects of these transformations have symbolic value in the mythical system and their precise meaning can be inferred from the qualities given these subjects in the narrative and from their position in the system of mythical oppositions.

The chart in figure 4.12 is identical in structure to the chart in figure 4.11 but it represents the mythical structure that can be discovered to underlie the parable of the good Samaritan. The ideal religious person who is symbolically opposed to the robbers does not appear in the narrative but can be inferred. The fundamental opposition in the parable of the good Samaritan is between order or the kingdom of God and chaos or the kingdom of Satan. The robbers are like the kingdom of Satan. The ideal religious person is like the kingdom of God. Though the kingdom of God and the kingdom of Satan cannot be mediated the ideal religious person and the robbers can. The Samaritan is like the ideal religious person insofar as he does good, but his state is like

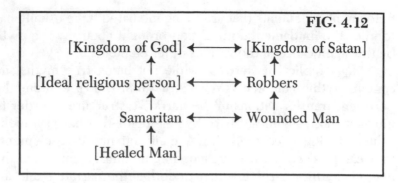

FIG. 4.12

[Kingdom of God] ←——→ [Kingdom of Satan]

[Ideal religious person] ←——→ Robbers

Samaritan ←——→ Wounded Man

[Healed Man]

that of the robbers—he is disordered, he is a heretical Jew worshiping away from Jerusalem.

Though the Samaritan provides the necessary mediation between the ideal religious person and the robbers, the distance between the Samaritan and the robbers, or between the Samaritan and the ideal religious person, is still great. Easier to mediate is the proportioned opposition between the Samaritan and the wounded man who had been placed in a state of chaos by the robbers. The Samaritan is healthy but disordered; he is not going anywhere. The wounded man is unhealthy but ordered; he is going somewhere (to Jericho). Like the scavenger in the example illustrated in figure 4.11, the healed man provides the necessary final mediation. Like the Samaritan he is healthy, like the wounded man he has direction in his life. The Samaritan, the wounded man, the ideal religious person, the robbers, the kingdom of heaven and the kingdom of Satan all fit together in the mythological structure that underlies the parable of the good Samaritan.

What has been described above is the kind of deep mythical structure that can be found in many biblical narratives. This basic mythical structure preexists the formation of myths or the composition of narratives that incorporate mythical elements. Uncovering its presence in the parable of the good Samaritan enables one to analyze consciously a level of meaning that is there, that truly has an effect, but that one otherwise might not consciously be aware of. The meaning, at this level, of the parable of the good Samaritan is that the ideal religious person is to the robbers as the Samaritan is to the wounded man. The Samaritan, in effect, acts like a truly religious person even though he has the same state as the robbers. Grasping this proportion involves an awareness of the cultural codes that underlie this text. The Samaritan is in a state of a chaos, a state of disorder. Samaritans are outside the pale of the truly religious person just as are the robbers. In terms of their state, there is no difference. The priest and the levite are ordered in their religious and societal lives, not chaotic, in the same way as the man going down from Jerusalem to Jericho is ordered in his activity.

This parable has a curious feature that is highlighted in a structuralist analysis, one which might not even be noticed apart from a structuralist perspective. The man is going down from Jerusalem to Jericho. The priest and the levite likewise are going down from Jerusalem to Jericho. The Samaritan, however, is undirected. Where he is coming from or where he is going is nowhere stated or even implied. The robbers too are undirected; they are just there. The Samaritan and the robbers have no directed movement. The man, the priest and the Levite do have direction; they are all going down from Jerusalem to Jericho.

The full semantic effect of the parable can only be appreciated by probing, as structuralists do, down through the various levels, down through the deep structures, so that one can see how the semantic effect of the parable is produced. When one gets down to the level of the deep mythical structure of this parable it is clear that what the parable does is challenge the truly (or traditionally) religious person. As long as the traditionally religious person does not venture outside the truly religious world and become irreligious, like the Samaritan, he cannot be symbolically identified with the truly religious person. He does not belong to the kingdom of God. It is not a matter of acting like the Samaritan; this parable is not an example story, i.e., one that encourages the helping of sick people by the roadside. There is a great deal more to it. It is a very fundamental parable of the kingdom that challenges traditional religious values.

What has been arrived at in this analysis is an aspect of the semantic universe that underlies the text. The goal of structuralism, as described in figures 4.4 and 4.5, is to uncover the deep structures that underlie a text in order to discover the deep system of convictions that is communicated by these deep structures. One of these convictions involves a challenge to traditional religious values. Even without structural analysis a person reading this parable can actually gain this sense of what the parable is saying. Most Christians have heard this parable many times and it has had an effect on them. It has done something to them, something like what has been described above. It has not been necessary to sit down and dig out the deep narrative structures or the deep mythical structures to figure out why it has the effect that it does have. Nevertheless it is the function of criticism to figure out how and why works of art or literature have the effects that they actually do have. Structuralism is simply performing its function as a form of criticism in figuring out how and why the parable of the good Samaritan has the effect that it actually does have.

The parable of the good Samaritan is a simple narrative with a limited number of narrative programs and a correspondingly small number of mythemes in its mythical paradigm. More complex narratives will have a far greater number of narrative programs and mythemes but the fundamental narrative and mythical structures will be the same.

6. MARCAN PASSION NARRATIVE

In Chapters 14 and 15 of Mark there are an enormous number of narrative programs, each involving a subject (S), an object (O) and a receiver (R). Of these, structural analysis has determined that thirty-four involve pertinent transformations, i.e., there exists within the narrative other programs with opposing transformations. The subjects of these programs therefore represent mythemes in the symbolic system, each one of which is opposed by a corresponding mytheme.

To illustrate something of what is involved, one small section of this symbolic system will be explained. Mark 15:45–46 contains three narrative programs that involve pertinent transformations.

15:45: And when he learned from the centurion that he was dead, he granted the body to Joseph.

15:46: And he bought a linen shroud, and taking him down, wrapped him in the linen shroud, and laid him in a tomb which had been hewn out of the rock; and he rolled a stone against the door of the tomb.

In Mark 15:45 Pilate (S) gives permission (O) to Joseph of Arimathea (R) to bury the body of Jesus. This program is a pertinent transformation because there is, in the narrative, an opposing transformation, i.e., in Mark 15:15 Pilate (S) gives satisfaction (O) to the crowd (R) which requests the release of Barabbas. In Mark 15:46 Joseph (S) gives non-cross (O) to Jesus (R), i.e., he removes Jesus' body from the cross. This too is a pertinent transformation because it is opposed to the transformation in Mark 15:24 where the soldiers (S) give the cross (O) to Jesus (R), i.e., they crucify him. Finally, again in Mark 15:46, Joseph (S) gives the shroud (O) to Jesus (R), a transformation opposed to the transformation in Mark 15:17 where the soldiers (S) give the purple cloak (O) to Jesus (R). The opposed narrative programs can be represented schematically as in figure 4.13.

These transformations are ordered according to the sequence in the narrative of the programs that manifest the positive values of the text, i.e., a respectful attitude toward Jesus. The opposing programs, which express abuses against Jesus, appear in no fixed sequential order in the text. What this analysis is moving toward is the mythical or symbolic system in which, as ex-

FIG. 4.13

```
        S       O       R
15:46 Joseph (shroud > Jesus)
                    15:17 Soldiers (purple cloak > Jesus)
                            S           O           R

15:46 Joseph (non-cross > Jesus)
                    15:24 Soldiers (crucifixion > Jesus)

15:45 Pilate (permission > Joseph)
                    15:15 Pilate (satisfaction > crowd)
```

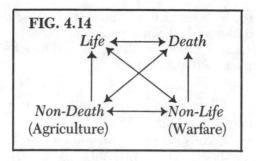

FIG. 4.14

Life ⟷ Death

Non-Death ⟷ Non-Life
(Agriculture)   (Warfare)

plained earlier, sequential order is unimportant. What is important in this system is the logical order among the symbols.

Two steps remain before one can determine what these opposed transformations reveal about the semantic universe that underlies the text. First, the symbolic value of the subject of each transformation needs to be determined. Second, the opposed symbols must be arranged in squares of opposition in order to perceive the full meaning effect of these symbols. The square of opposition used by structuralists is basically the same as the square of opposition which first appeared in Aristotle's treatise on logic, *Peri Hermenias* (On Interpretation). Figure 4.14 illustrates the oppositions among mythemes discussed earlier in this chapter. The diagonal opposites are contradictory while the horizontal opposites are contrary. In a narrative manifestation the opposed transformations correspond to oppositions of contradiction. In order, therefore, to achieve a semantic square of opposition one must shift the negative axis (the right hand column of figure 4.13) upward as in figure 4.15. If all the opposed transformations along these axes had been listed, a whole series of semantic squares would have been generated, each one of which

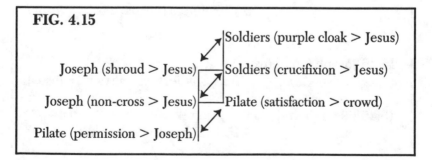

FIG. 4.15

Joseph (shroud > Jesus)   Soldiers (purple cloak > Jesus)

                                       Soldiers (crucifixion > Jesus)

Joseph (non-cross > Jesus)   Pilate (satisfaction > crowd)

Pilate (permission > Joseph)

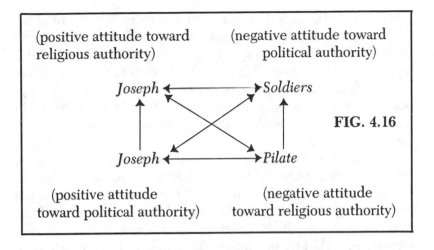

(positive attitude toward religious authority)   (negative attitude toward political authority)

Joseph ←————————→ *Soldiers*

Joseph ←————————→ *Pilate*

FIG. 4.16

(positive attitude toward political authority)   (negative attitude toward religious authority)

could then have been examined to determine its semantic effect. In the present abbreviated analysis only one complete square has been generated.

In the central square in figure 4.13 there are four subjects, Joseph, soldiers, Joseph and Pilate. Each one of these subjects is a symbol whose symbolic value can be inferred from pertinent features of the narrative. All of these subjects manifest various attitudes toward authority which yield the square with the symbolic values illustrated in figure 4.16. Joseph who wraps the body of Jesus in a shroud shows respect for Jesus' religious authority while the soldiers who crucify Jesus show contempt for the kingdom of the Jews, i.e., for his political authority. Joseph who takes Jesus' body from the cross with Pilate's permission shows respect or non-contempt for Pilate's political authority, while Pilate who turns Barabbas over to the crowds shows non-respect for Jesus' religious authority.

This square is only one of the many semantic squares that can be discerned in the Marcan passion narrative, squares which structuralists have systematically organized to reveal the semantic universe or system of convictions that underlies this text. The values represented by the symbols in figure 4.16 are actually secondary values but they are connected to other, more primary values that are found in the text. What this kind of structural analysis yields is the conclusion that beyond being a sequential narrative about the passion and death of Jesus, this text (Mk 14–15) also involves a mythical system that communicates the nature of authentic religious authority. The true nature of ultimate political/religious authority is not capable of being spelled out in straightforward, unambiguous language. This kind of authority involves values which, as ordinarily understood, are irreconcilably opposed. This kind of authority can therefore only be expressed in a manner that goes beyond ordinary human expression, i.e., in mythical language.

The author of the Marcan passion narrative was probably not consciously intending to discuss the idea of ultimate authority, yet this idea was an important part of the semantic universe, the system of convictions, that made possible the composition of this narrative. The mythical structure used was likewise not consciously intended by the author. This structure is, according to structuralists, part of the unconscious structuring capacity of every human. Through this structure the author's fundamental convictions about the true nature of religious/political authority entered into the full meaning effect of the passion narrative.

The reader of the passion narrative will usually sense that the text is communicating something about the true nature of religious/political authority. Such a reader, however, will normally be unable to formulate just what is being communicated and even less able to explain how it is being communicated. Structuralism fulfills its function as a form of criticism by first explaining how the text communicates and then attempting to express, as far as possible, what it is that the text communicates.

7. BEYOND STRUCTURALISM

Structuralism continues to be a significant form of biblical criticism with many scholars pursuing the structuralist goal of determining the invariant structures that are found in a text and from these structures describing the system of convictions that underlie the text. There are others, however, who once used the methodology of structuralism but have more recently left or gone beyond the presuppositions and methods of structuralism.

Jacques Derrida has challenged the philosophical presuppositions of structuralism, especially its notion of literary texts as signs which function by having determined and necessarily related signifiers and signifieds (see figures 4.4 and 4.5). For Derrida the signifier takes on greater importance and the precise meaning of the text can never be pinned down. Derrida's approach is known as deconstruction, for it is based on the conviction that the more one attempts to find meaning in a text the more the text deconstructs itself into various other possible meanings. In deconstructionist terms, the textual logic is confounded through the development of figurative tensions. Where structuralists consider a literary text to be a representation or an image that can be rendered intelligible in its full meaning effect by rigorous methods, Derrida maintains that the text is a representation with no single determined essence. Deconstruction has had little direct effect on biblical studies but other forms of post-structuralism have, especially those which emphasize the role of the reader.

Roland Barthes, an important figure in the early development of structuralist literary criticism, eventually became convinced that universal formal structures simply do not exist. He has since gone on to challenge the manner in which structuralists perceive literary objects suggesting that instead of viewing the text as an objective entity one should change the level of perception so that writing and reading are defined together.

Edgar McKnight agrees with Derrida that a text builds up a reality effect and simultaneously destroys that effect. He agrees, as well, with Derrida's concern to liberate language from fixed representational concepts. However, he goes beyond the negative aspects of Derrida's approach by insisting, as would Barthes, that texts do have a reality effect, an effect, however, that can only be grasped in the concrete act of reading. Post-structuralism, in at least some of its manifestations, is moving in the direction of the form of criticism to be discussed in the next chapter, reader-response criticism.

SUGGESTIONS FOR FURTHER READING

Calloud, J., "A Few Comments on Structural Semiotics: A Brief Explanation of a Method and Some Explanation of Procedures," *Semeia* 15 (1979) 51–83.

Crespy, G., "The Parable of the Good Samaritan: An Essay in Structural Research," *Semeia* 2 (1974) 27–50.

Derrida, J., *Dissemination*, translated, with an introduction and additional notes by B. Johnson (Chicago: University of Chicago, 1981).

Harari, J. (ed.), *Textual Strategies: Perspectives in Post-Structuralist Criticism* (Ithaca: Cornell University, 1979).

Kovacs, B., "Philosophical Foundations for Structuralism," *Semeia* 10 (1978) 85–105.

Lane, M., (ed.), *Introduction to Structuralism* (New York: Basic, 1970).

Lavers, A., *Roland Barthes: Structuralism and After* (Cambridge: Harvard University, 1982).

Leach, E., and D. A. Aycock, *Structuralist Interpretations of Biblical Myth* (Cambridge: Cambridge University, 1983).

McKnight, E., "Generative Poetics as New Testament Hermeneutics," *Semeia* 10 (1978) 107–121.

Patte, D., *Paul's Faith and the Power of the Gospel: A Structural Introduction to the Pauline Letters* (Philadelphia: Fortress, 1983).

Patte, D., *What Is Structural Exegesis?* (Philadelphia: Fortress, 1976).

Patte, D. and A. Patte, *Structural Exegesis: From Theory to Practice* (Philadelphia: Fortress, 1978).

Via, D. O., *Kerygma and Comedy in the New Testament: A Structuralist Approach to Hermeneutics* (Philadelphia: Fortress, 1975).

Chapter 5

READER-RESPONSE CRITICISM

Of the more recent types of criticism to come into use by biblical scholars the one that many consider to be the most promising is reader-response criticism. Beginning in the late 1960's and becoming more pronounced in the early 1970's a tendency has developed among secular literary critics to stress the reciprocal relation between the text and the reader as opposed to an earlier emphasis on the autonomy of the text. During the past decade new techniques developed by these literary critics have been used by biblical critics, especially in the study of biblical narratives, e.g., the Gospels and Acts.

1. TERMINOLOGY

The newly developed methodology used by literary critics when applied to biblical narratives is often referred to as narrative criticism, a specific application of this methodology that will be considered in the next chapter. This methodology, however, has applications to forms of literature other than narratives and is often, even when used to analyze narratives, referred to by the more general name, reader-response criticism. Frequently, however, biblical scholars often use the term literary criticism when they are speaking about reader-response criticism, or, in dealing with the Gospels, about narrative criticism.

The use of the term "literary criticism" is unfortunate for at least two reasons. First, the expression "literary criticism" has at least two meanings when it is used by biblical scholars. There is a type of biblical criticism known as literary criticism which has been around for a century and a half. There is, in addition, the type of biblical criticism presently under consideration, also known as literary criticism, which has just recently come on the scene. Why the confusion of terminology? As has been pointed out in previous chapters, there is little that is original in the critical techniques used by biblical scholars. Most of the methodologies used in biblical studies were first developed in some area of profane studies. When biblical scholars borrow a methodology from literary critics they refer to it simply as literary criticism.

When nineteenth century biblical scholars examined the problem of the sources of the Pentateuch and the Synoptic problem, they did so using techniques borrowed from the literary critics of their day known generally under the double name literary source criticism, sometimes referred to as source criticism, but quite often simply referred to as literary criticism. This is the methodology that was borrowed a hundred and fifty years ago. Today, biblical scholars are borrowing reader-response criticism from the literary critics. Because this methodology is what many literary critics are using today it too is often referred to simply as literary criticism.

A second reason why the use of the term "literary criticism" is unfortunate is because there are many other methodologies borrowed from literary critics other than reader-response criticism. Sometimes these other methodologies, when used by biblical critics, are referred to simply as literary criticism. Rhetorical criticism, for example, is a form of literary criticism applied to the Bible which is quite distinct not only from reader-response criticism but also from all the other types of criticism thus far discussed.

To avoid terminological problems the term "literary criticism" will be used to refer to literary criticism in general, embracing all methodologies borrowed from secular literary criticism. The term "reader-response criticism" will be used to refer to the specific, newly developed methodology presently under consideration. The term "narrative criticism" will be used to refer to reader-response criticism as it is used by biblical critics specifically in the study of biblical narrative, e.g., the Gospels and Acts.

2. READER ORIENTED CRITICISM

Reader-response criticism has been widely used among literary critics for about fifteen years. It actually began developing even longer ago but it was only about fifteen years ago that it began to achieve significant recognition. It has been used with increasing frequency ever since then, although there are still many literary critics who strongly resist it. It came on the scene as a reaction against, or even as a revolt against, the rigid objectivity of both Structuralism and the New Criticism.

2.1 The New Criticism

As mentioned in Chapter II, back in the 1940's an approach to literary criticism was developing in England and America which was then called and still is called the New Criticism. It was something that had newly come on the scene and was replacing all previous and thus discarded techniques of literary criticism.

A basic tenant of the New Criticism was objectivity. The New Critics rigorously avoided what they considered a major error of previous criticism, namely, looking into the author's subjective intention in order to determine the meaning of the text, i.e., asking the question "What did the author mean?" Significantly this question is precisely the question that was being asked by biblical critics using the historical-critical method, a method developed from previously used techniques of literary critics. Noteworthy as well is the fact that the development of the New Criticism was roughly contemporaneous with Pope Pius XII's encyclical in which he encouraged Catholic biblical scholars to do precisely what the New Critics were avoiding, i.e., seeking the intention of the author. What literary criticism is concerned about, according to the New Critics, is what can be found in the text itself using rigorous, objective methods.

The New Critics not only avoided seeking the intention of the author, but they also rejected any attempt to find the meaning of the text in the subjective perceptions of the reader. If someone were to make a comment like "I feel good about it" or "I like it" or "It made me a better person," the New Critics would say, "You can talk like that if you want to, but such comments have nothing to do with literary criticism." In 1949 it became current among the New Critics to consider anyone who introduced subjective interpretations as one who had committed what the New Critics called the affective fallacy. To allow anything that happens to the reader to enter into the understanding of the text is to distort the objective meaning of the text. The New Critics developed rigorous methods in the 1940's and 1950's for interpreting every work of literature, whether it be a novel or a poem or whatever else, by examining what could be found objectively in the text itself.

Why did the New Critics take the position they did? Part of the reason involved a philosophical concern for pure objectivity. Another part of the reason involved economics, or so it is alleged by some contemporary opponents of the New Critics. It was and, unfortunately, still is the case that funding for academic endeavors is more available if scholars can demonstrate that their methods are objective rather than subjective. There are actually many reasons why the New Criticism developed as it did. Most of the reasons, however, are connected with the fact that literary critics, like almost everyone else doing academic or scholarly work, had come under the influence of scientific positivism.

The success of the physical sciences in the nineteenth century had a tremendous impact on other disciplines in the twentieth century. Virtually every other discipline was compelled to adapt to the positivist conceptual framework out of which science operated. Scholars were faced with the choice of either adapting or being cast off to the periphery of serious study. If literature was to retain its position as a serious academic discipline it had to adapt to the positivist conceptual framework of the physical sciences. The New Critics responded to the demands of this conceptual framework by developing verifiable methods for drawing rigorous conclusions.

Reader-response critics are in open revolt against the New Critics. They feel that their discipline, literature, has been subjected to alien methodologies. They therefore go on the offensive and maintain that literature deals with subject matter that cannot be treated scientifically. One cannot put literature under a microscope and measure it like a molecule. Literature deals with human attitudes, with feelings. The result of a literary endeavor is in no way objectively verifiable.

What is it that a work of literature accomplishes? What a scientific experiment accomplishes can be measured with some kind of objective certitude. Can what a literary work accomplishes be measured with the same kind of rigorous objectivity? The New Critics tried to do just that. Reader-response critics, however, maintain that rigorous objectivity is impossible. Literature is not the kind of thing that can be measured objectively. Many reader-response critics would go even further and say that not only is the positivist conceptual framework not applicable to literature, it is really not even applicable to science. There are, in fact, serious problems in every discipline with the positivist conceptual framework.

All explanations of the world, including scientific explanations, are interpretations. Some would claim that ultimately there is no such thing as rigorous objectivity. Even today there are some physical scientists, especially in the field of theoretical physics, who are coming to the position that what was once thought to be a rigorous, objectively verifiable discipline is not that at all. Regardless of what might be said about other disciplines, literature certainly, according to reader-response critics, is not a discipline that is susceptible to objective verification.

2.2 Structuralism

The New Critics maintained that all that existed was the objective work itself and that it was in this objective work that objectively verifiable meaning was to be found. The historical-critical method used by biblical scholars, almost exclusively up to recent times, involved basically the same point of view. Though historical critics differed from the New Critics in searching for the intention of the author, they nevertheless maintained, along with the New Critics, that a given book of the Bible has an objective meaning and with their rigorous methodology they

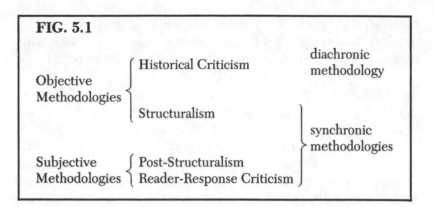

FIG. 5.1

could determine what that meaning is. Even structuralists, although they take a synchronic approach rather than a diachronic approach, have a similar attitude toward the written work. The work exists by itself, apart from the reader, and structuralists can dig into it with their methodology to find out what it is saying. Figure 5.1 illustrates the relationships among historical criticism, structuralism and reader-response criticism in terms of whether they are objective or subjective, diachronic or synchronic.

In recent years a number of scholars versed in the methodology of structuralism have turned to a form of reader-response criticism. Some, following the lead of Roland Barthes, feel it is simply not possible to discover the kind of rigorous objective structures that structuralists presuppose must exist. Others, like Gary Philips, insist that when studying the conceptual signified of a literary text one must consider pragmatics in addition to syntactics and semantics. According to this view the diagram of figure 4.5 in the last chapter would have to be redrawn as in figure 5.2. The symbolic meaning of the text can lead to a clear understanding of the system of convictions that underlies the text, but the full meaning of the conceptual signified includes the pragmatic effect of the text on the reader. Philips would not object to a structuralist study of the semantics of a text but he would object to any study of a text that, in principle, excluded the involvement of the reader.

Consider again the sound analogy that was used in the previous chapter. Suppose a group of people sitting in a room heard

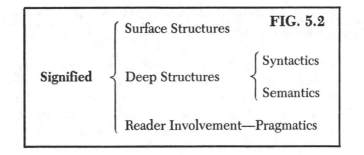

FIG. 5.2

Signified
- Surface Structures
- Deep Structures
  - Syntactics
  - Semantics
- Reader Involvement—Pragmatics

a large crashing sound. There are certain structures within all humans that would cause all of the people in that room to create with their ears and brains basically the same sound. They would all hear basically the same thing, but what does it mean? Is it a tree crashing in the woods? Is it an automobile accident? What is it? One might think it is one thing, another might think it is something else. Different people do not always interpret things the same way. What structuralists insist upon in their rigor is that there is an objective content. By analyzing the structure of the enunciation, by analyzing the cultural structures and by going down to the deep narrative structure and the deep mythical structures, one can come to the objective content of a literary work that will be the same for everyone.

For reader-response critics, however, the full meaning of literature is created by the reader. Literature is at least as subjective as sound. With sound there is a twofold subjectivity. First, the very sensation of sound is something created by the hearer, though it is probably the case, because of the structural similarity of sense organs, that all hearers of a given sound hear about the same thing. Second, the interpretations of and reactions to certain sounds can vary enormously from one hearer to another. While structuralists are willing to admit the first type of subjectivity into their analysis of literature, their presuppositions about the uniformity of deep structures renders the meaning of literature just as objective as it is for the New Critics.

Reader-response critics, in opposition to structuralists and other objectivist critics, maintain that it is simply not the case that there is a single objective meaning available to all. Wolfgang Iser, one of the foremost scholars studying profane literature by the methodology known as reader-response criticism, expresses the fundamental indeterminacy of literary meaning in a way that recalls the definition of sound.

> Communication in literature is a process set in motion and regulated not so much by a given code, but by a mutually restrictive and magnifying interaction between the explicit and the implicit, between revelation and concealment ("Interaction between Text and Reader," in *The Reader in the Text*, eds. S. Suleiman and I. Crosman [Princeton: Princeton University, 1980] 111).

Iser is suggesting that there is something more to the reception of the meaning of a literary work than simply decoding by means of universally held deep structures. What is in need of decoding by the reader is not entirely determined. The "waves" sent forth by a literary work are only partially defined. Their wave-like character consists precisely in the "interaction between the explicit and the implicit." The structure itself involves potentialities. Gaps that occur in the text are deliberate and essential. As a result, one and the same story can be actualized in a wide variety of ways by a variety of readers.

There is a great deal that a literary work provides and that the reader can figure out is really there, but there is also a great deal that the reader must supply in putting the literary work together and making it meaningful. Reader-response critics take the rather difficult position that there is no such thing as purely objective content apart from the meanings that are supplied by the reader. The historical-critical method can do a great deal about uncovering the history behind the text and the intention of the author. Structuralism can do a great deal about digging down beneath the text and uncovering the cultural codes and the narrative and mythical structures that are there. Ultimately, however, at least for reader-response critics, the full meaning of the text is supplied by the reader.

2.3 Biblical Studies

In the mid-1970's some biblical scholars started utilizing techniques developed by reader-response critics and brought into biblical studies the subjectivism that reader-response critics were insisting had to be part of literary criticism. The reason for applying this methodology to biblical studies is simple: the Bible is literature. If it is valid to use a given methodology on the works of Homer or Shakespeare or Mickey Spillane or any other work of literature, it is valid to use it on the Bible.

Borrowing methodologies from profane studies is what biblical critics had always done. The literary source criticism used by biblical scholars a hundred and fifty years ago was taken over from profane studies. The text criticism first applied to the Bible by the humanist Erasmus was taken over from profane studies. The allegorical method of biblical interpretation used at Alexandria, when it was the greatest center of Christian learning in the early centuries, was taken over from profane studies. There is a good pedigree for adopting in biblical studies methodologies that work in profane literature. Nevertheless, there has been tremendous resistance among scholars concerned about objectivity to using a methodology that suggests that the meaning of the biblical text is subjective, i.e., that it depends on the reader.

At the 1981 annual meeting of the Catholic Biblical Association there was a panel headed by Raymond Brown that made an impassioned plea for the retention of the historical-critical method as the mainstay of Catholic biblical studies. A fundamental concern expressed by members of that panel was that other methods being introduced were less certain, less objective than was the historical-critical method. Nevertheless, just as reader-response criticism has succeeded in profane literary studies, in recent years it has been achieving such success in biblical studies that many feel it is the wave of the future. Many serious Catholic biblical scholars are now wholeheartedly pursuing reader-response criticism.

3. CHARACTERISTICS OF
READER-RESPONSE CRITICISM

3.1 Literary Works as Bi-Polar

The point of departure for reader-response criticism is the conviction that a literary work is a virtual entity. A literary work is not something that exists complete by itself and that therefore can be looked at under a microscope. A literary work is a bi-polar virtual entity. A virtual entity is something which is capable of existing but which does not yet exist. Only when the two poles of a literary work are both operative does a literary work come into being. Every truly literary work has both an artistic pole and an aesthetic pole. The artistic pole is the accomplishment of the author, namely the piece of writing. The artistic pole is the artistic creation of the author. That, however, is simply one of the poles. The other pole, the aesthetic pole, is the work of the reader. Both of these poles are necessary. Without both of them operating, the literary work is simply a potentiality. Its potentiality becomes an actuality when both of these poles are operating, when a reader picks up the work of an author and actually reads it. In actually reading it, it comes into being. It is real, it has meaning, and it does something.

What happens when a reader picks up a literary work—when a Christian picks up a Gospel—is much more than what can be found on the printed page because the reader's imagination comes into play. The reader's imagination must come into play, for otherwise the literary work does not fully exist as a literary work. Using the author's text, the reader creates the literary work. The virtuality of the text is reduced to actuality. It is almost like a mound of unformed clay becoming a statue in the hands of an artist. The reader is the artist who reduces the potentiality of a written text to the actuality of a literary work. What many find objectionable in reader-response criticism is the fact that this aesthetic pole is different for every individual reader.

3.2 Creativity of the Reader

The subjective activity or the creative activity of the reader is what reduces the potentiality of a literary work to actuality. This subjective activity can vary from one reader to another. A literary work, therefore, has an infinite variety of meanings. One can never close the door on the possible meanings of a literary work.

The fact that bringing a literary work into being requires the activity of the reader is clear in the case of narratives. Any narrative that one reads, including the Gospel narratives, is a story. A story is, by its nature, sequential. It has a beginning, a middle, and an end. After a person has read a novel, or a short story, or a play, or a Gospel, or any section of any of these, that person can usually tell the story. That person did not, however, read the story. What that person read was the narrative discourse. Only after one reads the narrative discourse does one know the story. In fact, the reader creates the story in the sense that it is the reader who has to put it together.

The narrative discourse, the signifier of the literary work, does not lay out the entire time frame from beginning to end. What the narrative discourse usually does is to start with some significant event and then relate something that happened afterward, and then explain what happened afterward by relating something that happened a long time earlier, and what followed from that, and what one expected would happen much later on as a result of what had happened much earlier. In narrative discourses information is not laid out in the fashion of a bank TV monitor. With such a monitor the incidents related appear in their correct temporal sequence and the amount of time accorded to each incident is exactly proportioned to the amount of time involved in the incident. With narratives not only are events frequently related outside of their correct temporal sequence but some occurrences of very long duration are quickly summarized while some brief events are explained in the minutest detail.

The incident about the magi from the Gospel of Matthew can be used to illustrate what happens when one reads a narrative. Where does the story begin? That story begins when the magi see the star rising in the east and then depart for Palestine.

They go to Jerusalem and find out from Herod that the child has been born in Bethlehem and so on. Although the first thing that happens in the story is the star rising in the east, that is not the first thing that the Gospel narrative relates.

> Now when Jesus was born in Bethlehem of Judea in the days of Herod the king, behold, wise men from the East came to Jerusalem, saying, "Where is he who has been born king of the Jews? For we have seen his star in the East, and have come to worship him." When Herod the king heard this, he was troubled, and all Jerusalem with him; and assembling all the chief priests and scribes of the people, he inquired of them where the Christ was to be born. They told him, "In Bethlehem of Judea; for so it is written by the prophet" (Mt 2:1–5).

The first thing that the Gospel relates is that the magi come to Jerusalem. Only afterward does it explain why they have come to Jerusalem. They get to Jerusalem and then tell Herod not only what caused them to come, i.e., the star rising in the east, but also their purpose in coming, i.e., to pay homage to the new-born king of the Jews. The story, as it appears in the book, is actually here, there and everywhere. The reader has to take what is given on the printed page and put the story together. The reader's activity is necessarily involved in putting the story together, for authors quite deliberately do not simply list the events that happen in their correct chronological sequence.

Authors deliberately create artistic works that will involve the activity of the reader, that will tantalize the reader, tease the reader, challenge the reader, upset the reader, and force the reader to get into the text and do something with it. It is only by accepting the challenge of the author and working to put the story together that the reader gets something out of the text as he or she is reading it. The reader has to work at putting together the story, and in working to put together the story, the reader becomes involved, at the aesthetic pole, in creating the artistic work. Temporal sequence is only one of the many devices that authors use to involve the reader in the process of putting together the story, but it is one of the easiest to recognize.

Authors, in fact, use all kinds of strategies to involve the reader in the text. The text comes alive in the reading precisely because the reader is involved. The reader getting into a text is like a sports enthusiast getting into a ball game or a rock music enthusiast getting into a Springsteen concert. It is always possible to be a cool, passive, objective onlooker but the event will not have the same meaning as it would if one really became involved with it.

One of the strategies found in most if not all narratives involves the use of gaps. The question "How do you make a doughnut?" will often bring the response "You first take a hole and then . . ." Holes or gaps are almost essential for narrative communication. The author deliberately leaves gaps in the information supplied to the reader. The reader is then forced to fill in the gaps, at least tentatively, in order to make sense out of the narrative. Readers fill in these gaps by making assumptions, assumptions which quite often will subsequently be challenged by further information supplied by the author. The reader must then revise, reformulate or discard the assumption. By the end of the narrative the reader will have a complete picture in which what was supplied by the text was filled out by what was supplied and revised by the reader. Not every reader, however, will have the same picture.

One reader might conclude the reading of a given narrative with the assumption intact that a given character was tall while another reader might think the same character was short. It might be that the height of this character was unimportant, but were that the case readers would not even think about it. It is more likely that what was important was forcing the reader to think about the height of a given character. In the Gospel of Mark, for example, the text induces the reader to evaluate the various characters that appear and subsequently helps to clarify or refine that evaluation. Most readers will settle on a clear evaluation of the Pharisees that will remain rather consistent throughout the narrative. Their evaluation of the disciples will take some interesting twists and turns as the narrative unfolds but by the end of the narrative most readers will have arrived at much the same evaluation. The text seems to encourage a specific evaluation of the Pharisees and the disciples, but how is the reader to evaluate those characters who come to Jesus in faith looking for a miracle, receive a miracle and then disobey Jesus when he commands silence? The text certainly encourages the reader to supply an evaluation but never seems to help clarify it. Apparently all that is really important in this instance is the active involvement of the reader in making sense out of the narrative.

3.3 Indeterminacy of Both Text and Reader

As explained above there is indeterminacy or potentiality in the text, i.e., the activity of the reader is required to bring a literary work into being. It remains now to consider the more difficult idea that the reader is likewise indeterminate. It was pointed out earlier that, for reader-response critics, a literary work has both an artistic pole and an aesthetic pole. It comes into being when the two poles are both operating. When the author and what he has put into the text meets the reader making sense out of the text, the literary work comes into being. The text itself, however, already exists in potentiality. In much the same way, a reader, according to many reader-response critics, is a potentiality. The self is not a perfectly defined autonomous entity. The self is an indeterminacy that is always being determined. Choosing whether or how to actualize a given text is not as simple a matter as might first appear. In many ways choices are constrained or limited by indeterminacy. In a sense humans are not radically free.

3.3.1 American Freedom and the New Criticism

Radical freedom is an issue on which reader-response criticism stands very much at odds with the New Criticism. The idea of radical freedom, the ability of each individual person to choose his or her own destiny, is a very American idea, an idea that lies at the heart of the Jeffersonian concept of society on which America was built. The New Criticism was very American. In fact its origin was in America. It was rooted in the American concept of the autonomy of the self and the freedom of the self. Something of the fear of subjectivity that the New Critics had was rooted in this American concept of the freedom of the self. One cannot let an absolutely free person impose on the text any meaning he or she wants. The New Critics recognized both the autonomy of the text, and the freedom and the autonomy of the reader. For the enterprise of reading to make sense one had to insist that there was objective meaning in the text.

Robert Hilburn, the critic who wrote the article, mentioned in Chapter 1, on the rock music of Bruce Springsteen, suggested that Springsteen, in his album, *Born in the U.S.A.*, is trying to say something very profound. According to Hilburn, Springsteen is saying that "the absence of hope blurs the distinction between freedom and captivity." If this is what Springsteen is saying, he is not only saying something profound but he is also expressing a genuinely American concern. Apparently Springsteen is concerned that the present generation, because of its absence of hope, is really losing its freedom, unwittingly surrendering its freedom and falling into a kind of captivity. It is only by recapturing this hope in the American dream that the real distinction between freedom and captivity can be maintained and that the truly American ideal of the free, autonomous individual making his mark in the world can be achieved. Both Springsteen and the New Critics are committed to the American concept of the radically free, autonomous self.

Reader-response critics, on the other hand, reject both the autonomy of the text and the freedom and autonomy of the reader. Neither the text nor the reader is fixed and firm and complete in and of itself. The reader is not free. The reader is not a determined, autonomous, separate entity.

3.3.2 Peirce and the Cartesian Self

Many reader-response critics rely on the insights of the nineteenth century American philosopher Charles Sanders Peirce who opposed what he considered to be the Cartesian idea of an autonomous self. For René Descartes, the self was primary. "I think, therefore I am." One knows oneself first and then knows the rest of reality. The self has an independence and autonomy apart from the rest of reality. For Peirce, the self is not primary. It is not intuited directly. It is not independent or free. The self is perceived, like everything else, by inference. As words are signs, so too are thoughts, i.e., signs that signify something other than themselves. Just as the meaning of words and other signs outside of human minds are determined by the society that uses them, so too are thoughts dependent on the assumptions of the society to which people belong. The self that is perceived by in- ference from thoughts is not, as Descartes would have it, an au- tonomous, independent self, but a self that is already embedded in a social context.

Walter Benn Michaels, a reader-response critic, maintains that the self, like the literary work, is a text already embedded in a context, a community of interpretation or a system of signs. The self that freely constructs meaning (what the New Critics feared) is as illusory as a text that contains meanings independent of the reader's perceptual habits. The reader simply is not free to impose any meaning on a given text. This approach to literary criticism, however, opens up a serious question. If humans are not radically free is there such a thing as moral responsibility? This question is beyond the realm of literary criticism. It was, however, treated by the apostle Paul whose treatment of the question was much closer to Peirce and reader-response critics than to Descartes and the New Critics.

3.3.3 Pauline Freedom and Reader-Response Critics

Pauline Reader of Moses

Reader-response critics maintain that one must assume a specific role (that of the implied reader, to be discussed in the next chapter) in order to actualize a literary work. Furthermore, they maintain that one must either enter into the value system of the text or find oneself unable to cope with the text. In 2 Co- rinthians Paul writes,

> Yes, to this day whenever Moses is read a veil lies over their minds; but when a man turns to the Lord the veil is removed. Now the Lord is the Spirit, and where the Spirit of the Lord is, there is freedom. And we all, with unveiled face, behold- ing the glory of the Lord, are being changed into his likeness from one degree of glory to another; for this comes from the Lord who is the Spirit (2 Cor 3:15).

According to Paul the Jews are unable to read Moses. Why? Because their minds are veiled. They can read the words of the Pentateuch but they really cannot appreciate them. They are unable to assume the role called forth from them by the text. Christians, however, can. Why? Because Christians have the Spirit, because the very being of a Christian has been changed. Christians are being changed into God's likeness from one degree of glory to another. It is only by being changed into another being that Christians are capable of reading Moses with unveiled minds. The way reader-response criticism would express this idea is that Christians are capable of assuming the role called for by the text of the Pentateuch. Having been changed into God's likeness, they can become the reader of that text. Having been embedded in a new social context their selves are able to assume a role that the Jews, in their social context, were unable to assume.

Lack of Freedom

Reader-response critics also maintain that the individual self is not autonomous. Here too Paul is in agreement. One could say that Paul, like the reader-response critics is very un-American. What Paul means by freedom is not what Springsteen, or Thomas Jefferson, or the ancient Athenians meant by freedom. In Romans Paul wrote,

> But thanks be to God, that you who were once slaves of sin have become obedient from the heart to the standard of teaching to which you were committed, and, having been set free from sin, have become slaves of righteousness (Rom 6:17).

For Paul, there is no such thing as human autonomy, or radical human freedom in the American sense. All there is is slavery. It is simply a question of to whom one is enslaved. Either one is a slave of sin or one is a slave of righteousness. Either one is a slave of Satan or one is a slave of God. There is no middle ground, there is no human autonomy in the American, Jeffersonian sense. Though Paul rejects the idea of human autonomy he does not reject moral responsibility. Moral responsibility, however, is viewed from a different perspective than that of the Greek philosopher. For Paul, moral responsibility is viewed from the perspective of the value system that dominates one's existence. Whatever that value system is, it constrains human activity. Certain choices and activities are possible while others are impossible. Paul describes existence under two different value systems in Chapters 7 and 8 of his Letter to the Romans. Reader-response critics are not involved in discussions about moral behavior but they would insist, as Paul does, that one is always in the grip of some value system. For this reason one is able to assume the role demanded of the reader of certain literary works but not of others.

Paul would not say, as Springsteen might, that the absence of hope blurs the distinction between freedom and captivity. What Paul would say is that in the absence of hope one is a slave of sin rather than a slave of God. True freedom consists in true slavery. They are not to be distinguished, they are to be united. Only a slave of righteousness has the freedom to read Moses in the light of God's salvific plan for mankind.

4. READER-RESPONSE CRITICISM AND THE BIBLE

Is it possible to adopt a methodology for biblical criticism which regards the text as indeterminate and open to a multiplicity of meanings? Does not such an approach do violence to the notion of the Bible as a sacred text? The above comments about Paul's insights should ease any concern about unbridled subjectivity destroying the sacredness of the text. The analyses and illustrations in Chapters VI and VII should provide concrete evidence of the validity of a method which regards the text as a potentiality. The discussions about canonical criticism in Chapter VIII and the place of Scripture in the Church in Chapter IX will respond to the question about the possibility of a sacred text being open to a variety of possible meanings.

SUGGESTIONS FOR FURTHER READING

Eco, U., *The Role of the Reader* (Bloomington: Indiana University, 1979).

Crossan, J. D., "A Metamodel for Polyvalent Narration," *Semeia* 9 (1977) 105–147.

Iser, W., *The Act of Reading* (Baltimore: Johns Hopkins University, 1978).

Mailloux, S., "Reader-Response Criticism?" *Genre* 10 (1977) 413–431.

Oller, J., "On the Relation between Syntax, Semantics and Pragmatics," *Linguistics* 83 (1972) 43–55.

Peirce, C. S., *Philosophical Writings of Peirce*, selected and edited with an introduction by J. Buchler (New York: Dover, 1955), especially Chapter 16, "Some Consequences of Four Incapacities," 228–250.

Phillips, G. A., " 'This Is a Hard Saying. Who Can Be Listener to It?': Creating a Reader in John 6," *Semeia* 26 (1983) 23–56.

Savon, D., *An Introduction to C. S. Peirce's Semiotics* (Toronto: Victoria University, 1976).

Suleiman, S. K., and I. Crosman (eds.), *The Reader in the Text* (Princeton: Princeton University, 1980).

Tompkins, J. P. (ed.), *Reader-Response Criticism* (Baltimore: Johns Hopkins University, 1980).

Wittig, S., "A Theory of Multiple Meanings," *Semeia* 9 (1977) 75–103.

Chapter 6

NARRATIVE CRITICISM

Over the past decade the methodology of reader-response criticism has been utilized in biblical criticism, especially in the study of narratives, e.g., the Gospels and Acts. A highly developed methodology for studying biblical narratives from the perspective of reader involvement has been taken over from secular literary critics and is usually referred to as narrative criticism.

The charts in figures 6.1 and 6.2 illustrate some of the factors involved in the methodology of narrative criticism. Figure 6.1 illustrates the fact that narrative critics recognize, as do structuralists, that narratives are signs that have both a signifier and a signified. The signifier is the narrative discourse itself. The signified is the content of the story. The content of the story, however, does not come into being apart from the activity of the reader. It is not enough, therefore, to analyze the syntactic and semantic components of the text in order to arrive at the full meaning effect. One must also analyze the pragmatic component. There are, for narrative critics, many factors involved in producing that story that involve the activity of the reader. The story is not something that is completely defined by the text itself, objectively perceivable and objectively verifiable. Figure 6.2 illustrates some of the factors that are involved in producing the signification of a narrative text.

What narrative critics do is analyze each of the factors appearing in figure 6.2 in order to appreciate how the full meaning effect of the text is produced. Traditional literary critics had concentrated on the narrative content, studying such things as plot

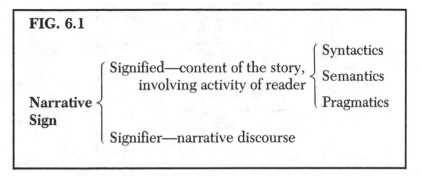

FIG. 6.1

Narrative Sign
- Signified—content of the story, involving activity of reader
  - Syntactics
  - Semantics
  - Pragmatics
- Signifier—narrative discourse

and character. Reader-response critics do not ignore these elements but they consider them in the larger context of the relationships among authors, texts and readers. In the analysis of biblical narratives one of the most important factors, as will be explained below, is the implied reader.

1. AUTHORS AND READERS

The terminology of reader-response criticism or narrative criticism can be a bit confusing because different writers use different terms, e.g., terms like textual enunciator and scriptive enunciator are sometimes used instead of implied author and real author. The terms used in figure 6.2 and in the following discussion seem, however, to be winning general acceptance. Even with terminological variations there is general agreement among narrative critics about the existence and importance of the six "persons" illustrated in figure 6.2.

1.1 Real Authors and Readers

The words author and reader are modified in the diagram by the words real and implied. The real author is the real person who wrote the given literary work, e.g., the Gospel of Matthew. The real reader is the person who happens to pick it up and read this work. In figure 6.2 these two persons are depicted as existing in the real world outside of and independent of the text. The diagram is intended to indicate the fact that though there was a real flesh and blood person who authored the text just as there are

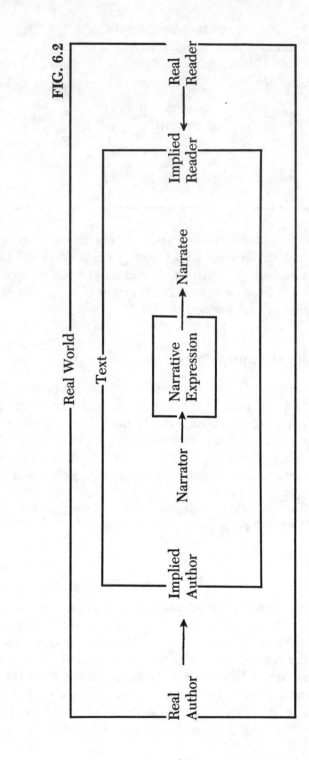

FIG. 6.2

94

real flesh and blood persons who pick up the text and become its readers, the text itself exists apart from both real author and real reader.

1.2 Implied Author

One of the significant contributions of narrative criticism is the idea of the implied author, not a real flesh and blood person but rather a literary entity that is to be found in the text. The implied author is the authorial person discoverable in the text. Every work of literature has an implied author that is distinguishable from the real author. One can read a sonnet of Shakespeare and, just from that single sonnet, can glean an understanding of the person who wrote it. What is gleaned, however, is not an understanding of a full person. One does not get an image of the real Shakespeare. What one gets are the feelings, the values, the concerns and whatever is available that comes to expression in this text, i.e., whatever the real author decides to make the governing values, or ideology, or concerns, or objectives of this text. An important thing to note is that one and the same real author can write a wide variety of different works, each one of which could have a very different implied author.

The possibility of having diverse implied authors with one and the same real author is actually what is involved in much of the discussion about the authorship of the pastoral letters. Did Paul write the pastoral letters? Almost everyone today says no, observing that the concerns and values and ideology behind the pastorals are clearly very different from the concerns and values and ideology behind Romans, Galatians and Corinthians. The few scholars who hold for Pauline authorship argue that the differences can be accounted for because at the time Paul would have written the pastorals he was considerably older, his ideas had matured and he was tired and worn out. In sum he was writing as a different person. In effect these scholars are saying that the implied author of the pastorals is indeed very different from the implied author of Romans, but the real author of both was one and the same person. Although this particular argument could have a measure of plausibility, there are sufficient other grounds justifying the position of the majority of scholars who insist that even the real authors had to be different. If, however, one compares Galatians and 1 Corinthians one can see in the language and style used that the same person wrote both of these letters. Although almost everybody agrees that one and the same person wrote Galatians and 1 Corinthians, the values espoused and the concerns expressed in these two letters are very different. In some ways they are almost diametrically opposed. Paul is telling the Galatians, "You are free; live your freedom to the fullest." The same Paul then tells the Corinthians, "Take it easy. You are indeed free, but freedom can be pushed too far." These two letters clearly have different implied authors.

1.3 Implied Reader

The implied author is something discernible in the text and has its counterpart, the implied reader. The implied reader is the reader implied by the text. What the text does is it provides directives to a reader. The reader is the one who has to put the text together. There are certain presuppositions made by the text concerning the reader. There are certain directives given to the reader, certain expectations made of the reader, all regarding the reader's aesthetic function of putting the text together. The implied reader, in terms of capabilities and ideology, is to be found, like the implied author, within the text. The implied reader, however, does not perfectly parallel the implied author insofar as there are aspects of the implied reader not entirely defined by the text. Nevertheless the implied reader is distinct from the real reader, the real flesh and blood person who picks up the text and reads it.

The role of the implied reader will vary from reader to reader because of the indeterminacy of both the reader and the text. The text is a potentiality which calls forth from its readers certain commitments and values, but no individual reader perfectly perceives and fulfills the role required by the text, if indeed that role could even be unambiguously defined. At the same time the reader is a potentiality. Each individual reader brings a distinct and imperfect personality to bear upon the text. All humans are imperfect in one way or another. All have loose ends and, to a certain degree, really do not know who they are.

What literature does for its readers, at least what good literature does, is that it helps them to know themselves. To the extent that people can become implied readers, to the extent that people can fulfill the role presupposed by a text, to that extent people make a strong commitment of their very persons to the act of reading and come to know themselves more deeply. Reading the Gospel of Matthew involves much more than an objective analysis of a fully defined text. It involves a deep personal commitment to the act of reading which will enable that act of reading to have a transforming effect on one's life.

Sometimes a reader approaching a text is challenged by the text to assume a particular role but decides instead to reject that role. Perhaps the reader simply does not like the person that the implied author seems to require one to become in order to read the text. The reader can either plow through the text and end up quite disgusted with the whole enterprise, or else, after a few pages, simply put the text away. Very often, even in the case of good literature, that can happen. One simply decides not to accept the role that is called for by the text, i.e., decides not to become the implied reader of the text. That can happen when the ideology presupposed by the text is, in some way, undesirable, i.e., involves characteristics one simply does not want to adopt.

Choosing whether or not to assume the role of an implied reader, however, is not as simple as the above comments would seem to suggest. Human choices are limited or constrained by the human indeterminacy mentioned earlier. In addition, the self of the real reader is already partially constituted within a given social and cultural context. As Paul maintains, there is no such thing as radical human autonomy. All humans are slaves, either to sin or to righteousness.

Becoming an implied reader involves something very similar to this Pauline notion. Becoming an implied reader involves becoming a slave of the text, becoming a slave of the ideology involved in the text. Most reader-response critics would agree that if one does not become a slave of the text, share the ideology of the text, one simply cannot read it. Some people are unable to read Dante, some people are unable to read Milton. Why? Because they do not have the ideology presupposed by the text. A Christian can pick up the sacred literature of the Hindus and can read it as an historical critic might, but probably will not be able to make sense of it as a Hindu might because a Christian reader would have difficulty assuming the role of the implied reader of the text. Only a believing Christian can read the New Testament. A scientist can pick up the Bible and subject it to various kinds of analysis, but only a believer can assume the role of the implied reader of a biblical text.

Once, during my graduate studies, a student in one of my classes shared with me her anguish over difficulties she was having with her dissertation director. She, a Moslem, was writing on some aspect of the Koran under the direction of a Christian professor. The professor, it appears, was merely insisting that she be rigorously objective. She, however, found that she could only satisfy his demands by suspending her religious beliefs while working on her dissertation. According to reader-response critics, there are some beliefs that cannot be momentarily suspended just as some beliefs cannot be momentarily assumed. Had she been a Christian or had her director been a Moslem neither would have noticed that beliefs had not been suspended and both might have falsely assumed that some kind of rigorous objectivity was being pursued.

2. NARRATORS AND NARRATEES

If the text is a narrative, whether it is a novel, or a short story, or a Gospel, or some other kind of narrative, there is also to be found in the text a narrator. The narrator is the person who tells the story. Narrative criticism attaches almost the same importance to the study of the narrator as redaction criticism attaches to the study of the theology of the redactor. For the redaction critic the theology of the redactor is the key to understanding what the redactor intends to accomplish by editing the materials in a given way. For the narrative critic the person and activity of the narrator is often the key to understanding the true nature and purpose of a given narrative text.

One thing that literary criticism studies is the variety of narrative techniques that can be used. Sometimes one of the characters in the story narrates the story in the first person. "I was awakened in the middle of the night by a shrill cry and went out to find my neighbor strangled to death." A story that begins in this way has what is said to be a first person narrator. Sometimes the first person who narrates the story is the hero or heroine of the story. Sometimes the person who tells the story is simply an observer who sees things happening, perhaps the secretary, the servant, or the chauffeur.

2.1 Narrator and Implied Author

Sometimes the narration is done in the third person. This type of narration is the most common. With this type of narration one can be tempted to think that it is the author or, using the distinction made above, the implied author who is telling the story. Such is not the case. The narrator is always a creation of the implied author who endows the narrator with characteristics and abilities and uses this fictive entity to bring about the artistic effect of the narrative.

The significance of the distinction between the implied author and the narrator can be illustrated by considering the manner in which historical critics analyzed the speeches in the Acts of the Apostles. Earlier historical critics using the methodology or form criticism considered these speeches to be paradigm examples of early Christian preaching. More recent historical critics using the methodology of redaction criticism see in the speeches an opportunity for the author to state his theology. Both of these approaches isolate the speeches from their narrative context. The implied author has created the entire narrative context but within that context has placed a narrator who relates words and deeds that are significant for the flow of the narrative. Peter's speech in Acts 3 may or may not bear some relation to actual preaching that occurred in the early Church. It may or may not give expression to the peculiar theology of the author. However, it certainly does address the situation of the audience in the narrative, the populace of Jerusalem that has recently rejected Jesus. The narrator relates this speech because it pertains to the flow of the narrative. Such is the primary focus of narrative criticism. All other considerations are secondary.

When the narrator under consideration, as is the case in all four Gospels, is a third person narrator, the question of the narrator's competence becomes far more significant. If the narrator created by the implied author happens to be one of the characters in the story, all he or she can see, and therefore tell about, is what he or she is present to. If, however, the implied author creates a narrator who is omniscient, and tells the story in the third person, then this narrator is almost God-like, can see everything extended in time and space, and can even see into the deep inner thoughts and feelings of all of the characters in the story. Such a narrator can see how everything is related and can then choose what to reveal in the narration. Just how competent the narrator is is entirely up to the creative genius of the implied author. There are all kinds of degrees less than full omniscience that the implied author can grant to the narrator. The narrator of the Gospel of John possesses almost the omniscience of God while the narrator of the Gospel of Matthew is far less gifted. While the former is unrestricted by time and space and can perceive the inner thoughts and feelings of humans, the latter is restricted to the time and space of Jesus' life and ministry and rarely has greater insights than could be attributed to an intelligent observer on the scene.

2.2 Narratees and Implied Reader

Narrators have long been studied. Something that has not been studied all that much until very recently is the narratee, the counterpart of the narrator. To whom does the narrator tell the story? Not to the real reader, not even to the implied reader of the text. What the implied reader reads is the text in its entirety. The implied reader reads what the implied author created, namely a narrator telling the story to a narratee. That is basically what was diagrammed in figure 6.2 earlier in this chapter. The narrator tells the story to the narratee. The implied author is that aspect, that set of values and concerns, that creates this work.

The implied reader is that set of values that is capable of bringing this work to its aesthetic completion.

What about this narratee? The narratee is totally defined by the work. Sometimes, in some few works, the narratee, the person to whom the narrator tells the story, is actually a character in the story. One could have a novel in which an older man is telling his grandson about what happened fifty years ago. In this case the aged grandfather is the narrator telling about his youth, and the young grandson is the narratee. This kind of thing can happen, but in most cases the narratee is unnamed and does not appear anywhere in the story. It is actually possible to read many narratives without ever thinking there is such a thing as a narratee or to assume that the real reader is the narratee. According to this common assumption, the real author composed a narrative in which someone (the narrator) tells the story to the reader. For contemporary narrative critics, however, the narratee is a fictive element entirely defined by the text and distinct from both the implied reader and the real reader. Like the narrator, the narratee has specific functions that are carried out according to the competencies granted by the implied author.

One can determine a great deal about the narratee by noticing the kinds of things the narrator says. Some narratees are virtual idiots. They know absolutely nothing and have to have everything spelled out for them in detail. This kind of narratee is what reader-response critics would call a zero degree narratee. A zero degree narratee has certain minimal competencies like an ability to speak the language but little else. The role of the narratee is very much like that of a very important member of Napoleon's staff. Whenever Napoleon was about to send orders to his generals in the field he would write the orders out and hand them to an idiot who would then read them. He would then ask the idiot to explain the orders. If the idiot could explain them, Napoleon would then send the orders out to his generals. Why did he go through all this trouble? He went through all that trouble because he was brilliant enough to recognize that even brilliant people are not always unambiguous. It is all too easy to compose a memo that one thinks is absolutely plain and clear only to discover later that the recipient interpreted it differently from what was intended. Obviously the memo was not that unambiguous. Many wars were lost because generals misunderstood the directives of the commander-in-chief. Much of Napoleon's success depended upon this idiot.

The narratee is very much like Napoleon's idiot, i.e., a person with minimal competencies. It is to the narratee that the narrator lays out the details of the story. The implied reader, however, is the one who puts the story together. The implied reader listens to the narrator spelling out all these things to the narratee. The narratee is often little more than a marginal idiot who can understand everything that is said. It is the implied reader who has the competency to put all of the information together, to create the narrative world.

3. NARRATIVE WORLD

3.1 Relation to Real World

The narrative world is not the real world. The real world in which real people live and move and have their being is unbounded in space and time. The world of the narration may resemble the real world but it differs in at least one significant respect. It is a limited world with a well defined horizon. In the real world all events and existents, no matter how far separated in time and space, are somehow connected. A poet once expressed this interconnectedness with the line, "Pick a daisy and move a star." The same is true of the narrative world except that the interconnectedness is limited to the finite space and time of the narrative world which does not connect directly with the real world. Because of the finiteness and interconnectedness of the narrative world the implied reader is able to put together the whole story. At the end of the narration the implied reader will have a reasonably clear picture of this well defined, circumscribed, narrative world.

3.2 Gaps in the Narration

An important element in every narrative that the implied reader must deal with are the gaps, the things left unsaid. The implied author is very careful not to have the narrator function like one of those video cameras that banks use, cameras that record absolutely everything from the moment the bank opens until the moment the bank closes. That is not what happens in the narration. One never receives a step by step, sequential presentation of everything. One is given the important things. These important things are carefully arranged, with the arrangement highlighting some events, subordinating others, relating things from one time period to things in another time period. The whole narrative work is carefully laid out by the implied author who has his narrator tell things in certain ways, telling them in such a way that the marginally competent narratee can understand them and also so that the implied reader can, upon overhearing this narrator/narratee explanation, piece together the narrative world.

What the implied reader pieces together, however, is not entirely objective. It is not something that will be the same for everyone who reads the narrative. To illustrate this non-objectivity, consider one area in which reader-response critics differ profoundly from the New Critics. According to the New Critics, Hamlet, or any other character in any other work of fiction, is simply a word on a piece of paper. He is not a person. He is not even a fictive person, because a person is a full human being. All Hamlet is is a word that appears in the narrative, a word that appears many times, a word to which is attributed many personal characteristics, but which still is not a full person. If the book does not indicate what color that character's hair is or what color that character's eyes are or how tall that character is, then that character has no color hair, has no color eyes, has no height. A person would have to have these things. However, in a literary work viewed as the New Critics would view it, as something that is objectively analyzable, characters are not persons. They are simply whatever the printed page indicates they are.

Reader-response critics regard the position of the New Critics as inadequate. The position of the New Critics is based on the presuppositions of their objectivist methodology and not on the real experience of real readers. Real readers know that characters are persons, that Hamlet is a full person, that Tom Jones is a full person, that every character one meets in narratives is a full person. Even though all one has to go on is what is on the printed page, readers are quite adept at supplying the rest. The implied reader is able to reconstruct the story world by filling in the gaps, by filling in the things that are not spelled out in detail. Among the things that are filled out in the reading of narratives are characters. The implied reader fills them out to make of them real people, not real live people, but real people in the sense that they have everything that a real person has. They have hair, or they are bald. If they have hair, then their hair has a color, and if they have eyes, then their eyes have a color. They have a height. They have a weight. They have shape. They have texture. They have everything that human beings have, and if it is not spelled out on the printed page, then the imagination of the implied reader supplies it.

What implied authors do is that they compel the implied reader, by the artistic techniques they use, to round things out and to fill things out. The implied reader is drawn into the process, filling out what is left unsaid and thereby creating the work and bringing to completion the meaning effect of the literary work. The full meaning of a literary work is, therefore, in some sense subjective. Just as the implied author is that aspect of the real author that comes to expression in the work, in a similar way the implied reader is the role that the real reader is called on by the work to fulfill. The implied reader brings the literary work into being by assuming the role required by the text and in so doing receives from the text the growth in self-understanding that the text intends to communicate.

4. VALUE SYSTEMS

A reader who picks up the Gospel of Matthew is called upon to fulfill the role of the implied reader of the Gospel of Matthew. That is quite a different role from the role of the implied reader of a detective story. There are different values, there are different presuppositions, there are different competencies that are called forth from a reader who sets about to read the Gospel of Matthew than there would be for one who tries to read a detective story. The implied reader is the activity of the reader in this specific work. As mentioned earlier, however, the implied reader is not wholly defined by the work, as is the implied author, for the implied reader is the real reader who actualizes the work, and different real readers can actualize one and the same work in many different ways.

4.1 Structuralism

Many narrative critics find the methodology of structuralism to be helpful in determining the value system of the implied author of a text, i.e., the semantic universe of the text. Others are suspicious of the validity of the structuralist presuppositions and also find the scope of the structuralist methodology to be severely limited. As a result most narrative critics prefer to glean the value system presupposed by a work from whatever indications there are in the text at any level.

4.2 Ideal Reader

Another feature of narratives that is discussed by reader-response critics is the ideal reader. "Ideal reader" is a term that some people have used but that others prefer not to use. Some people have used this term to mean the reader totally defined by the text who does perfectly what the text wants this reader to do. This term first came into use when reader-response critics were still operating within the endeavor of maintaining the pure objectivity of the New Critics and the structuralists. Today, most reader-response critics have cast objectivity aside and have recognized that the reader is involved in creating meaning. As a result, many reader-response critics simply do not like to use this term "ideal reader." Some, however, do use it to refer to that aspect of the implied reader that is wholly described and defined by the text, that amalgam of presuppositions, ethical values, competencies, beliefs, that are presupposed on the part of the reader by the text. The ideal reader, however, is not a full person. The ideal reader is simply an aspect of the implied reader.

The implied reader is that full person who actualizes the text, utilizing the competencies defined by the text for the ideal reader. To the extent that the real reader fulfills the role of the implied reader, to that extent the text works the way the text should. Because, however, the implied reader is not entirely defined by the text, the text will work differently in every different real reader.

5. VALIDITY OF THIS METHODOLOGY
   IN THE STUDY OF THE GOSPELS

When narrative criticism first became introduced into Gospel studies many questioned its appropriateness, and many still do. Narrative criticism can reasonably be used for analyzing profane literature. It is especially effective for analyzing novels, which are very clearly narratives, where there is obviously a story being told. However, are the Gospels narratives in the same way that novels are narratives? One of the things that reader-response critics have done, and done very effectively, is that they have focused on the narrator that is very clearly manifested in each of the Gospels. It is true, as the historical-critical method has shown, that the Gospels come out of an historical progression in which historical events were put into various forms and collected and handed on and adapted according to the needs of the tradition, and then collected into shorter units, and then composed into sources, and finally these sources were used to compose the Gospels. Granting all of this, one can still not ignore the fact that if one takes the Gospel of Mark and reads it from Chapter 1 verse 1 to Chapter 16 verse 8 one is reading the words of a narrator. There is a single narrative voice from beginning to end. The historical processes leading up to the Gospel of Mark may have been long and complex, but the final work is a single, unified narrative, having all the characteristics of a genuine narrative.

Using the techniques utilized in profane studies, analyzing the language of the narrator, the perspective of the narrator, the competence of the narrator, the psychological insights of the narrator, one cannot escape concluding that there is in the Gospel of Mark one and the same narrator who speaks from beginning to end. One can similarly discover a single narrator for each of the other three Gospels, the Gospel of Matthew, the Gospel of Luke and the Gospel of John. One thing that can be noticed is that the point of view of the narrator, the point of view from which the narrator tells the story, differs considerably from one Gospel to the next. The competence of the narrator differs considerably from one Gospel to the next. The narrator of the Gospel of John is nearly omniscient, with the omniscience of God, whereas, as shall be pointed out in the next chapter, the narrator of the Gospel of Matthew has a much more limited perspective. Matthew's narrator has some insights into what people are thinking or feeling, but not all that much. The narrator of the Gospel of Matthew is much more limited in his ability to know things in a superhuman way. The perspective, the point of view, from which the Gospel of Mark is told is very clearly the perspective of Jesus. The perspective from which the Gospel of Matthew is told is very clearly the perspective of God the Father. It is a different perspective in each but in each the perspective is consistent from beginning to end.

Narrative critics, such as Norman Petersen, have subjected the topic of point of view to detailed analysis. Petersen has distinguished four planes on which the particular point of view of a given work can be discerned: the ideological plane, the phraseological plane, the spatial/temporal plane and the plane of psychology. Though each of the four Gospels is different from the other Gospels, each of the Gospels manifests an internally consistent point of view on each of these planes.

These and other considerations, which have been worked out in great detail in the past few years, have led biblical scholars to realize that narrative criticism or reader-response criticism is a valid method to use in studying the Gospels. Just as there is, in each of the Gospels, a narrator, so also each Gospel has its narratee. Usually the narratee is unmentioned, unnamed, and almost invisible except in the Gospel of Luke. Who is the narratee in the Gospel of Luke? Theophilus! He is named right in the beginning. That is the person to whom the narrator is telling the story. Theophilus is a fictive person very similar to Veronica. Who is Veronica? She is the person who wiped the face of Jesus in the stations of the cross, receiving on her cloth an image of Jesus' face. Her name, Vera icon, was given to her to indicate her role in the story. Vera icon means "true image." Who is Theophilus? Theophilus means "lover of God." "Lover of God" characterizes the narratee of Luke's Gospel. More than being simply a marginal idiot, the narratee of the Gospel of Luke is characterized in the very first verses as a lover of God. This characterization of the narratee should influence how one appreciates the manner in which the narrator communicates.

Narrative criticism is a methodology that is capable of considering aspects of biblical narratives that previous forms of criticism have not adequately explored. It considers how the real author has utilized a set of values and concerns in creating a narrative work, a narrative work which involves the telling of a story by a narrator to narratee, a telling that is observed by an implied reader who is compelled to put the story world together. Certain competencies, certain values are required of the implied reader, and to the extent that the real reader assumes the role called forth for the implied reader, to that extent the real reader will receive what the text is supposed to give, although it can be different for each individual real reader.

The focus in the next chapter will be on the implied reader, especially on that aspect of the implied reader that is wholly defined by the text. The implied reader will be considered specifically with regard to the Gospel of Matthew, and an attempt will be made to draw out some further implications about the methodology of narrative criticism.

SUGGESTIONS FOR FURTHER READING

Chatman, S., *Story and Discourse* (Ithaca: Cornell University, 1978).

Culpepper, R. A., *The Anatomy of the Fourth Gospel* (Philadelphia: Fortress, 1983).

Iser, W., *The Implied Reader* (Baltimore: Johns Hopkins University, 1974).

Iser, W., "Narrative Strategies as a Means of Communication," in *Interpretation of Narrative* (eds. M. J. Valdes and O. J. Miller; Toronto: University of Toronto, 1978) 100–117.

Lanser, S., *The Narrative Act* (Princeton: Princeton University, 1981).

Petersen, N., *Literary Criticism for New Testament Critics* (Philadelphia: Fortress, 1978).

Petersen, N., " 'Point of View' in Mark's Narrative," *Semeia* 12 (1978) 97–121.

Prince, G., "Notes towards a Categorization of Fictional Narratees," *Genre* 4 (1971) 100–105.

Rhoads, D., "Narrative Criticism and the Gospel of Mark," *Journal of the American Academy of Religion* 50 (1982) 411–434.

Rhoads, D., and D. Michie, *Mark as Story: An Introduction to the Narrative of a Gospel* (Philadelphia: Fortress, 1982).

Rimmon-Kenan, S., *Narrative Fiction* (New York: Methuen, 1983).

Chapter 7

THE READER OF MATTHEW'S GOSPEL

In Chapter VI the various readers of a literary work, as analyzed by narrative criticism, were distinguished. The real reader is the actual flesh and blood person who picks up the text and reads. The implied reader is the specific role the real reader assumes in coming to grips with the text, a role that involves assuming certain presuppositions, values, insights and abilities implied by the text. It is only by assuming the role demanded by the text that the real reader is able to make sense out of the text or, in the terminology of narrative criticism, to actualize what is merely potential in the text. Unlike the implied author who is to be found entirely within the text, the implied reader involves both the role presupposed by the text and the specific realization of that role by a given real reader. In this chapter, however, the main focus will be on indications within the Gospel of Matthew that specify the role to be assumed by the implied reader of that text.

1. TEXTUAL PRESUPPOSITIONS

In considering the competencies which the text of the Gospel of Matthew presupposes on the part of its readers it is important to distinguish carefully between the narration in which the only voice heard is that of the narrator and the literary work which is the artistic creation of the implied author. The narrator is a creation of the implied author who speaks to another of the

110

implied author's creations, the narratee. The implied reader is the one who, by following the narration and appreciating its deeper implications, is able to bring the literary work into being. Generally very little is presupposed on the part of the narratee. Much more is presupposed of the implied reader. It is useful, however, to consider what the Gospel of Matthew presupposes on the part of its narratee before considering how much more is expected of the implied reader.

1.1 Narratee

As was pointed out in Chapter VI the narratee is often times a marginal idiot, so the text frequently presupposes very little. The text always presupposes, on the part of the narratee, a knowledge of the language that is used and the meanings of the sign system of communication that is used. The narratee does not necessarily understand all of the connotations of the language but he certainly understands the denotations of the language. The narratee can read English or can read Greek or whatever language the text is written in. That is presupposed. He knows the grammatical system. Furthermore, the narratee has the ability to reason, he has certain logical abilities and can follow the basic sequential argument of the text. The narratee has this ability, but the narratee is ignorant of the story. The narratee's role is specifically to be totally dependent on the narrator. He only knows, with respect to the story, what the narrator tells him, unless there are some other indications that he is more than a zero degree narratee. There are, in fact, some such indications in the Gospel of Matthew. The narrator, for example, frequently refers to the sacred literature of the Jews without explaining what it is or why it is so important. The narrator clearly presupposes that his narratee, the person to whom he is speaking, is familiar with this literature and understands its importance.

For the most part, narratees are incapable of value judgments. All they do is follow the story, and follow the logic that is provided them by the narrator. They simply listen to the narrator using their minimal competencies. An interesting aspect of the Gospel of Matthew is the use of various titles for Jesus. Most of the titles are carefully explained by the narrator to the narratee, e.g., Immanuel, Son of God, Christ and Son of David. The narrator presupposes only a very general knowledge of the scriptural background of these titles. What these titles mean is quite clear to the reader of Matthew's Gospel because they are presented in a way that is clear to the minimally competent narratee. The same, however, is not the case with the expression "Son of Man." The narrator never explains the meaning of this expression. Apparently the narratee does not need to understand this expression in order to follow the logic of the story. The implied reader, however, must come to grips with this expression in order to appreciate the literary work as a whole.

1.2 Implied Reader

The implied reader needs to be much more competent. The implied reader has to know the connotations of the language as well as the denotations. For example, in the parable of the good Samaritan all that is presupposed on the part of the narratee is that he can listen to the story. The narrator tells the story and supplies enough information for a marginal idiot to be able to repeat the story. That is what the narratee could do. The implied reader, however, knows the connotations and therefore can infer the mythical system that lies behind the story. The implied reader knows what a Samaritan is in the context of the culture of the time and therefore can see the symbolic value of a Samaritan and can infer the mythical system that is thereby connoted.

Furthermore, the implied reader knows something of the story, which is both a help and a hindrance. There are, behind the Gospels, historical truths. Apart from pure fairy-tales, almost any narrative has some real history behind it. The presence of real history in a text can be both a help and a hindrance because if the reader knows certain true historical events this knowledge can, on the one hand, help the reader get into the story more, but it can also, on the other hand, distort or disturb the reader's appreciation of the story especially when the author is taking liberties with historical events or with objective truths. Frequently the implied author will bend over backward to insist upon his version. When one sees the implied author doing this, one can then say that the implied author is clearly alluding to competencies presumed to be found in the implied reader. The implied author assumes that the implied reader already knows something about the topic being treated and therefore the implied author must bend over backward to bring the implied reader's understanding into line with the world of the story.

1.3 Story World

For the narratee the story world is the only world that exists. For the implied reader the real world is what really exists but this world must be temporarily abandoned in order to involve oneself in the world of the story. Such a temporary abandonment is both possible and necessary for the appreciation of narrative literature unlike the impossibility of abandoning the fundamental value system that controls one's existence. There is an interesting line, to use a somewhat contemporary illustration, in Samuel Becket's *Lot*. The line says, "Sam's other married daughter, Kate, age 21 years, a fine girl . . . but a bleeder." Anyone with a medical knowledge of the condition known as hemophilia should be troubled by this line. The implied author, assuming that at least some of his readers would possess this troubling knowledge, used a device quite rare in fictional works, a footnote. The footnote reads: "Hemophilia is, like enlargement of the prostate, an exclusively male disorder, but not in this work."

The implied author is taking liberties with objective reality. Women are not bleeders; but he, for his purposes, wants a woman to be a bleeder so he makes her a bleeder in this work and he sticks a footnote in to make sure that the implied reader is able to accept the fact that in this work, for the purposes of the implied author, a woman can be a bleeder. In effect the implied author is saying to the implied reader, "Just accept this unreal fact and let us get on with the story." The interesting point is the way he has to bend over backward to deal with what he assumes the implied reader knows.

Similar things happen in the Gospel of Matthew. Among other things this Gospel confuses, or lumps together, the various sects of the Jews. In the story of John the Baptist, the Pharisees and the Sadducees come to John (Mt 3:7). Historical critics have done all kinds of interesting things with this particular line as they have with similar lines elsewhere in the Gospel. The fact of the matter is that at the time John the Baptist was preaching one would never have seen Pharisees and Sadducees coming together from Jerusalem to the Jordan to see him. They were diametrically opposed to one another, but not in the Gospel of Matthew.

The story world of the Gospel of Matthew is not the real world but neither is it the story world of Mark. The implied author of Matthew presumes that his readers have some familiarity with the Gospel of Mark and is careful to insist on his story world as distinct from that of the earlier Gospel. Redaction critics have noticed numerous places where Matthew has consciously and with consistency changed passages that were taken from Mark, explaining these changes as indications of the theology of Matthew. Narrative critics would explain many of these changes as indicative of the different story worlds of Mark and Matthew. In Matthew's story world Jesus' behavior is more divine from the outset of his public life and his true identity as Son of God is recognized during that public life. Matthew therefore inserts a protest from John the Baptist into the baptism story and changes Mark's statement that Jesus could work no miracles in his home town to a statement that he did work no miracles there.

Even more significant for subsequent considerations are the changes Matthew makes in his presentation of the disciples. In Mark's story world the disciples are presented as failures who consistently misunderstand the true identity of Jesus and the significance of his activity. In Matthew's story world the disciples have a much more positive and powerful role to play. In the walking on the water incident the disciples of Mark's story fail to understand while the disciples of Matthew's story confess Jesus as the Son of God.

> And when evening came, the boat was out on the sea, and he was alone on the land. And he saw that they were distressed in rowing, for the wind was against them. And about the fourth watch of the night he came to them, walking on the

sea. He meant to pass by them, but when they saw him walking on the sea, they thought it was a ghost, and cried out; for they all saw him and were terrified. But immediately he spoke to them and said, "Take heart, it is I; have no fear." And he got into the boat with them and the wind ceased. And they were utterly astounded, for they did not understand about the loaves, but their hearts were hardened (Mk 6:47–52).

And when they got into the boat, the wind ceased. And those in the boat worshiped him, saying, "Truly you are the Son of God" (Mt 14:32–33).

What is happening in these and other passages of Matthew's Gospel is that the implied reader is being led to accept its peculiar story world. The implied reader is also being eased into the role that must be assumed in order to get into the story world of the Gospel of Matthew. The implied reader is being asked to leave aside any preconditions and simply to accept the story world of the Gospel of Matthew, so that what the Gospel of Matthew is intended to do can be done.

2. READING THE GOSPEL OF MATTHEW

The following discussion will consider what happens to the implied reader and what this reader does while reading through the initial chapters of the Gospel of Matthew, thereby bringing the Gospel of Matthew into being.

2.1 Genealogy

The Gospel of Matthew begins with the genealogy. The genealogy has a whole list of names that many people tend to rush through in order to get on with the story. The genealogy, however, is quite significant for the literary work as a whole. One can usually assume with truly good literature that nothing is inserted that is meaningless. One would like to assume that the Gospel of Matthew is good literature. The genealogy is indeed a long list of names but there are elements in that list that stand out like sore thumbs, e.g., the women.

And Judah the father of Perez and Zerah by *Tamar* (Mt 1:3).

And Salmon the father of Boaz by *Rahab*, and Boaz the father of Obed by *Ruth* (Mt 1:5).

And David was the father of Solomon by *the wife of Uriah* (Mt 1:6).

The women of the genealogy are precisely the kind of thing that reader-response criticism focuses on, things that strike one as unusual, things that one has to stop and deal with. It is in places like this that the reader is being pulled into the text and forced to think. "What does this mean? Why is this here? How am I to reconstruct the world where all of this fits together and makes sense?" The implied reader is the person who is required to be able to put together all of these things and make sense out of all of them. The implied author sticks things in there that jar and jolt and tease and upset and confuse and force the reader to come to grips with them. The women of the genealogy are one such confusing item.

The implied reader of Matthew's Gospel does not expect women to be in the genealogy. The implied author deliberately puts four of them in there. Why? What are they doing there? The implied reader does not know. It can, however, be inferred from the text that one is here dealing with a competency presumed by the text on the part of the implied reader. According to this presumed competency the implied reader would notice that something was strange about the presence of women and would therefore be forced to do something with it. At first all the implied reader can do is hold this unusual information in his mind and read on, expecting that somehow it will start to make sense. In the whole context of Matthew's Gospel eventually it does, for it prepares the reader for subsequent irregularities in the Gospel story. The most notable of these is the birth of Jesus to the Virgin Mary, but there are many other incidents prepared for by the women of the genealogy such as the role of the Canaanite woman in extending Jesus' mission to Gentiles (Mt 15:22–28). From the start, however, the women in the genealogy are a very significant element in getting the reader into the text and forcing the reader to deal with its problems.

2.2 Birth Story

The next section in Matthew's Gospel is the birth story. As mentioned in Chapter IV, this story is a simple narrative that follows the same pattern that can be found in the parable of the good Samaritan. The birth story begins:

> Now the birth of Jesus Christ took place in this way. When his mother Mary had been betrothed to Joseph, before they came together she was found to be with child of the Holy Spirit; and her husband Joseph, being a just man and unwilling to put her to shame, resolved to divorce her quietly (Mt 1:18–19).

As the story continues, the angel comes in the dream and allays Joseph's fears. He then takes Mary as his wife and the child is born and given the name Jesus.

This simple narrative can be analyzed according to a variety of methodologies. Using the historical-critical method and attempting to recover the historical progression that led up to the text, one would ask a whole series of questions. Why was this story inserted at this point in the Gospel? How was the story adapted in order to have it fit in at this point? What was the form of the story before it was adapted for Matthew's Gospel? What specific need in the life of the early community was filled by this pre-Matthean story? Where did the community get this story, i.e., what were its sources and what models (e.g., Old Testament models) were used? Finally, what actually happened at the birth of Jesus? Historical critics generally agree, in response to this last question, that almost nothing in the story is historically reliable other than the names of Joseph, Mary and Jesus and possibly the fact that Mary was a virgin, a fact that is independently attested to in the very different birth story of Luke's Gospel.

The same narrative can also be analyzed according to the

methodology of structuralism by uncovering the deep narrative structure found in this narrative and then, by discerning the pertinent transformations, arriving at the even deeper mythological structure that underlies the narrative. In Chapter IV it was observed that this story adheres to the same basic narrative structure found in Russian folk tales and also found in the parable of the good Samaritan. An intended order is disrupted, someone is mandated to restore that order, and finally the order is restored. Joseph decides not to take Mary as his wife, an angel is sent to persuade him to do so, and finally he takes Mary as his wife.

One could further analyze this story using structuralist methods to list all of the narrative programs, determine the primary and polemical axes, locate the pertinent narrative transformations and finally arrive at the mythological oppositions which the story is intended to mediate. In Chapter IV it was observed that the mythical structure according to which the various oppositions, life/death, agriculture/warfare, herbivores/beasts of prey, were analyzed was actually the same basic structure that was found in the parable of the good Samaritan, where the fundamental oppositions were the kingdom of God and the kingdom of Satan. One might suspect that a similar mythological structure could be found in the birth story of Matthew where, perhaps, the fundamental opposition would be between God and man and the ultimate mediation was provided by Joseph the chaste spouse. Joseph the chaste spouse would then be the most significant element in the story. It would then be a story not so much about the birth of Jesus and not so much about Mary, but about Joseph, the chaste spouse, and how Joseph the chaste spouse is what provides the ultimate mediation between God and man.

Narrative critics, however, would take a different approach to the analysis of this story. They would agree with the synchronic aspect of the structuralist analysis. They would agree as well that it is possible to analyze the narrative structure and also the mythical structure underlying this story. They would disagree, however, with the structuralist presupposition that there are fixed structures underlying all narratives and disagree as well with the structuralist attempt to uncover meaning in the text apart from the involvement of the reader. For narrative critics what is of paramount importance is how the implied reader makes sense out of the text.

Unlike the narratee who understands the denotations of the words and follows the logic of the text, the implied reader appreciates the connotations of the words and images used. He is aware as well of the need for myths to help people cope with the various oppositions that confront them and can sense in this story deep mythical values. Far more important than the precise mythical structure that underlies this story is the narrative critic's appreciation of what this story indicates about the implied reader and how this story enables the implied reader to appreciate the Gospel as a whole.

The implied reader of Matthew's Gospel knows the specific Christian concerns that make it necessary to have a myth that will provide the Christian with a tangible way to overcome the radical opposition of God and man. The implied reader of Matthew's Gospel has a need for this myth because unlike most of the people in the then civilized world the reader presupposed by Matthew's Gospel is a monotheist. For a pagan polytheist there is no infinite gulf between God and man. Gods are all over the place, and though they are somehow superior to men, they are by no means infinite and transcendent as was the one God of contemporary Judaism and Christianity. Only a true monotheist could perceive the infinite gulf that separates God and man. Christians, however, believed that this infinite gulf was overcome in the God-man, Jesus. Myths, like the one underlying the birth story, provided Christians with a tangible means of expressing their belief that this radical opposition had been overcome.

2.3 Jesus in Matthew

For the implied reader of Matthew's Gospel, Jesus is the Son of God. This is something that the implied reader knows. He has come to accept this truth, but he needs to have an easy way of handling it, of thinking about it with a human, creaturely, material imagination. The birth story fulfills this need. Mark's Gospel, on the other hand, is very different from Matthew's. Mark's Gospel presents Jesus as the Son of God, but it is something that

Mark's Gospel develops. The ultimate challenge of Mark's Gospel is to bring the reader to an awareness that this indeed is what Jesus is and to force the reader to do something with this idea. That is pretty much where Mark's Gospel ends, with the reader thrown up against the wall. "How am I going to deal with this idea that Jesus is God's Son?" The centurion at the foot of the cross is the first human being to recognize Jesus as the Son of God. Shortly thereafter the Gospel ends with the reader left to his own devices to try to handle this humanly incomprehensible idea.

Matthew's Gospel is quite different. Matthew's Gospel presupposes that the Christian believes that Jesus is the Son of God. The Gospel opens up with a story that gives the reader a myth by which to handle this belief more easily. That is what myths do—they provide a way to handle difficult things, like beliefs, that are a necessary part of one's life situation. This myth functions, at the outset, by enabling the reader to handle the idea that Jesus is God's Son. As the birth and infancy stories proceed, the reader encounters various other myths or mythical structures that enable the reader to handle things the reader is going to have to handle to get into the Gospel, to piece together the Gospel story. By looking at the narrative structures, and the myths that underlie them, one can glean a great deal of information about the kind of reader that is presupposed by the text.

3. DISCIPLES IN MATTHEW

As one moves on in the Gospel, one comes to a very important set of characters, the disciples, a set of characters who bear a special relationship to the Father. These characters, as will be explained below, are decisive for the involvement of the implied reader in bringing into being and being affected by the Gospel of Matthew.

3.1 First Impression

One of the things that is extremely important in any narrative is the attitude that the implied author evokes from the implied reader toward a character or a set of characters. In the infancy stories, for example, the implied author has carefully orchestrated his presentation of Herod to make sure that the reader has a very negative attitude toward Herod. The disciples, however, are deliberately brought on the scene in such a way that the reader has a positive attitude toward them. Subsequently, however, the disciples tend to fluctuate, and the reader is led to wonder about whether they are to be perceived in a good or in a not so good light. Again, it is very different in the Gospel of Mark. In the Gospel of Mark they are bad, they are stupid, they are ignorant, and, in the end, they desert Jesus. In Matthew the situation is not so clear-cut. The implied author of Matthew, in a way, plays with the disciples, and plays with the implied reader, and also with the implied reader's attitude toward the disciples.

3.2 Their Father

One of the things that the Gospel of Matthew very deliberately does in the initial presentation of the disciples is that it introduces them in the company of their human father. The section introducing the first four disciples moves toward the climactic final verse concerning James and John,

> Immediately they left the boat and their father, and followed him (Mt 4:22).

The passage focuses on the fact that they left their human father in order to follow Jesus. Why did they have to leave their human father? The implied reader asks this question but does not yet have the answer.

In the very next chapter, Jesus goes up on the mountain and delivers the Sermon on the Mount to the disciples (Mt 5–7). In that sermon he repeatedly speaks about "your Father."

> Let your light so shine before men, that they may see your good works and give glory to your Father who is in heaven (Mt 5:16).

> Look at the birds of the air: they neither sow nor reap nor
> gather into barns, and yet your heavenly Father feeds them
> (Mt 7:26).

About whom is he talking? He is talking about his own Father
who is also "your Father," and therefore can be called "our Father," in the form that the Lord's Prayer takes in the Gospel of
Matthew (Mt 6:9). The disciples left their human father and are
now brought into a new relationship with Jesus' Father.

3.3 Second Person Pronoun

Another literary device that is quite pronounced in the Sermon on the Mount is the use of the second person plural personal
pronoun. When the narrator reports words of Jesus in which Jesus refers to "you," to whom is he referring? This usage is found
not only in the Sermon on the Mount (Mt 5–7) but also in the
four other major discourses that are generally recognized as significant elements in Matthew's Gospel (Mt 10; 13; 18; 24–25).
When the narrator relates these discourses with Jesus using
"you," the implied author is invariably using a technique designed to involve the implied reader in the text. The careful use
of the word "you" is especially evident in the third discourse (Mt
13). This discourse, unlike all the others, can be neatly divided
into two halves in the first half of which a group of characters
known as the crowds are very much in evidence. In the second
half, however, the disciples alone are present with Jesus. What
is significant is that throughout the discourse Jesus consistently
refers to the crowds as "them" and to the disciples as "you." This
again is a device designed to bring the implied reader into the
text, enticing this reader to identify with a particular group of
characters, the disciples, with their ups and downs, their fluctuations, their challenges.

3.4 Reader Identification

The implied reader cannot help wondering about the disciples. As the implied reader becomes more involved with the

text in the process of putting the story together he is investing more of himself in the text. As he invests more of himself in the text he inevitably tries to see himself in the text.

3.4.1 Reader Puzzlement

As the implied reader follows the clues provided by the text in putting the story together he wonders about whether or not to identify with the disciples. Are they good? Are they bad? What are they? At one point the disciples were severely criticized.

> And then the disciples of John came to him, saying "Why do we and the Pharisees fast, but your disciples do not fast?" (Mt 9:14).

The disciples of John were suggesting that something was wrong with Jesus' disciples and were making a plausible case with which the implied reader might be inclined to agree. Jesus, however, stood up for his disciples. Jesus replied to the disciples of John,

> Can the wedding guests mourn as long as the bridegroom is with them? The days will come when the bridegroom is taken away from them, and then they will fast (Mt 9:15).

Jesus was, in effect, insisting that there was nothing wrong with the disciples' behavior.

A few chapters later Jesus again stood up for the disciples. This time they had not merely failed to do something good (like fasting) but they had clearly broken the Jewish law.

> At that time Jesus went through the grainfields on the sabbath; his disciples were hungry, and they began to pluck heads of grain and to eat. But when the Pharisees saw it, they said to him, "Look, your disciples are doing what is not lawful to do on the sabbath" (Mt 12:1–2).

Jesus, however, turned on the Pharisees and denounced them by saying, in effect, that if the disciples had broken the sabbath law, you people, i.e., the Pharisees, were far worse.

And if you had known what this means, "I desire mercy, and
not sacrifice," you would not have condemned the guiltless.
For the Son of man is lord of the sabbath (Mt 12:7–8).

What is significant is that Jesus consistently stood up for the disciples even when their behavior was less than exemplary and open to criticism. In designing the narrative in this way, the implied author is reassuring the implied reader that it is okay to identify with the disciples in spite of any misgivings that the text may have prompted.

3.4.2 Mother and Brothers

One of the most important passages for this process whereby the implied reader comes to identify with the disciples occurs just before Jesus began the parable discourse.

And stretching out his hand toward his disciples, he said,
"Here are my mother and my brothers! For whoever does
the will of my Father in heaven is my brother, and sister, and
mother" (Mt 12:49).

This passage is very different from the parallel passage that occurs in Mark. In Mark the reference is not to the disciples but to "those who sat about" (Mk 3:34), a group that includes people which the Gospel of Matthew sharply distinguishes from the disciples. One of the things that is extremely important in narrative criticism is to read each Gospel on its own terms and not be confused or influenced by what goes on in other Gospels. Although the Gospel of Mark is doing something quite different in this passage, the Gospel of Matthew uses this passage specifically to focus on the disciples and their role in achieving the overall purpose of the Gospel, i.e., involving the implied reader in making sense out of the text by identifying with the disciples.

3.4.3 Johannine Thunderbolt

Another significant passage for seeing how the text of the Gospel of Matthew elicits the involvement of the implied reader is the passage often referred to as the Johannine Thunderbolt.

The label itself is indicative of the problems that historical critics have had in interpreting this passage. Narrative criticism, however, can shed considerable light on its role and function in the Gospel as a whole.

> At that time Jesus declared, "I thank thee, Father, Lord of heaven and earth, that thou hast hidden these things from the wise and understanding and revealed them to babes; yea, Father, for such was thy gracious will. All things have been delivered to me by my Father; and no one knows the Father except the Son and anyone to whom the Son chooses to reveal him. Come to me, all who labor and are heavy laden, and I will give you rest. Take my yoke upon you, and learn from me; for I am gentle and lowly in heart, and you will find rest for your souls. For my yoke is easy, and my burden is light" (Mt 11:25–30).

The terminology here is so Johannine that people practicing the historical-critical method, those who try to explain the Gospels in terms of source criticism, form criticism, and redaction criticism, wonder where the passage came from and what it is doing in Matthew's Gospel. It is indeed an extraordinary passage. It is extraordinary, however, because it is the single passage that most perfectly establishes the disciples in the Father/son relationship that has been alluded to since the Sermon on the Mount. It is also at this point in the Gospel that the implied reader sees himself in that same Father/son relationship and is finally able to identify with the disciples in that relationship. As he reads through Chapters 11 and 12, leading up to the central chapter, Chapter 13, the implied reader should be getting into the text more and more. It is at this point, at the Johannine Thunderbolt, that the implied reader can see himself clearly in the role of the disciples, even with their fluctuations, their successes, their failures.

4. PURPOSE OF MATTHEW'S GOSPEL

The purpose of Matthew's Gospel is to challenge the reader to assume the role of the disciples, a role which is very demanding. As one reads the whole Gospel one can see that incredible challenges are brought to bear on the implied reader.

4.1 Disciples

The disciples are presented in the Gospel of Matthew as committed followers of Jesus whose faith is weak and whose behavior is often less than desirable. The story, however, as pieced together by the implied reader, shows the disciples gradually facing up to their deficiencies and becoming more faithful and responsible followers of Jesus. The implied reader who sees himself in the role of the disciples is confronted with his own deficiencies and challenged to deal with them. In order to read this text and to accept the challenges it evokes, it is necessary that the reader be a believing Christian, one who is part of a believing community and accepts the basic tenets of Christianity. Such a person can read this text, recognize and accept the role he is being challenged to assume and thereby deepen his own self-identity through the reading of the text. Such a person will come away from the text with a fuller appreciation of his or her identity as a Christian.

4.2 Readers

How a specific individual reader will accept this role will vary from one reader to another. How well, or poorly, one can fulfill what the text presupposes of the implied reader will vary from one reader to another, from one Christian to another. There are actually two areas in which, though one might read the Gospel of Matthew a thousand times, one can never exhaust its potentialities. One area involves one's ability to fulfill the requirements of the implied reader. Each time one comes back to the text, one comes back more and more like the reader presupposed by the text. Each time one reads the Gospel one sees something of what is expected of the implied reader. To the extent that one can fulfill these expectations in one's self-understanding, to that extent one can read the text and take up the challenge of the text and deepen one's own self-understanding.

The progression, however, is without limit, for no Christian will ever be the perfect implied reader of Matthew's Gospel.

The other area involves the role of the implied reader. The implied reader is much more than that which is defined by the text. The implied reader is that whole person who, by fulfilling what is required by the text, is then able to bring the text into being as a complete work of art. What the implied reader is challenged to do is to identify with the disciples, and to take up the challenge that is laid out to the disciples in becoming better people, in becoming better Christians. That is the role of the implied reader, which involves not only having the competencies of the implied reader, but also reducing them to some kind of actuality. How one actualizes the challenges taken up from the text will vary from person to person but one thing is certain—no one will ever perfectly actualize all of the challenges brought forth in the Gospel of Matthew.

4.3 Referential Fallacy

One thing that reader-response critics are very insistent on is that the referential fallacy should be avoided. Though there are all kinds of fallacies that critics warn against, only two of them have been mentioned in this book, the affective fallacy and the referential fallacy. The affective fallacy was warned against by the New Critics but reader-response critics regard it as no fallacy at all. According to reader-response critics, literature is operative only when the reader's subjectivity enters into the meaning of the text. To reject subjective interpretation as a fallacy (the affective fallacy) would be, for reader-response critics, to deny the very essence of literature.

The referential fallacy, however, is quite a different matter. To whom do the various events and existents of a literary work refer? To whom, for example, do the disciples of Matthew's Gospel refer? Historical critics, at one point in time, tried to analyze the disciples in terms of the disciples of Jesus' day, and to analyze the Pharisees and Sadducees, and so on, in terms of those people in Jesus' day, because, obviously, that is what the text is referring to, the life of Jesus and the people that were around at his time.

As the historical-critical method developed, and especially with the onset of redaction criticism, critics began to suggest that what the author of the Gospel of Matthew was talking about was the Church of Matthew's day. This suggestion helped explain why the author of the Gospel of Matthew could confuse the Pharisees and Sadducees. By the time of the composition of the Gospel the various parties of the Jews had all but disappeared. The author is therefore simply speaking globally of these people in the terminology of Jesus' day, but is actually referring to the Judaism of his own day, the Judaism of the rabbis of Jamnia. In Matthew's Gospel the Pharisees, the scribes, the Sadducees and the high priest simply refer to the leaders of the Jews at the end of the first century, the rabbis of Jamnia.

Similarly, historical critics would maintain, the disciples do not refer directly to the disciples of Jesus' day, but rather to the leaders of the Church of Matthew's day, whoever might be in a position of leadership. Unfortunately this reconstruction does not really work out. One can read the work of many redaction critics who maintain that the disciples refer to the leaders of the Church, but one will also find other redaction critics who say that they do not refer to the leaders of the Church so much as to Christians in general. Complicating the matter is the problem of the crowds. To whom do the crowds refer? Many critics suggest that the disciples refer to the leaders, the crowds refer to the people, and the relationship between the disciples and the crowds is the relationship between the leaders of the Church and the people in the Church in Matthew's day. The inability of redaction critics to discover a clear reference for the characters of Matthew's Gospel suggests that such cannot be done and perhaps should not be done.

Reader-response critics would say that all of these efforts are examples of the referential fallacy. The elements in the narrative do not refer to the real world. The narrative is a sign. What is on the printed page is the signifier, and it signifies a content, a story. What it refers to, what the disciples on a printed page of the Gospel of Matthew refer to, is the disciples of Matthew's story world. It is a whole world in and of itself, a contained world, a defined world. It is to this world that the disciples refer. The implied reader is expected to enter into the story world of Matthew's Gospel and to be moved by that story world, affected by that story world, rather than being sidetracked by committing the referential fallacy and trying to figure out whether the disciples of the Gospel refer to the disciples of Jesus' day or the Church of Matthew's day or the leaders of the Church of Matthew's day. The disciples refer to none of these. Their direct reference is only to the story world of the Gospel of Matthew. The reader is challenged to assume the role of the implied reader of that text. The implied reader of that text, possessing the presumed competencies, will, by following the cues of the text, identify with the disciples and be challenged to a deeper self-understanding through that identification.

To reject the referential fallacy is not to say that the Gospel of Matthew has nothing to do with the Church of Matthew's day or with any of the persons in that Church. Rejecting the referential fallacy merely involves rejecting an overly narrow interpretation of the text. The direct reference of all of the events and existents of the Gospel of Matthew is to the story world of that Gospel. Entering into that story world has a great deal of meaning for everyone in the Church in every age. The approach of reader-response criticism has a great deal of meaning for how the Scriptures, in general, function in the Church today.

5. READERS AS MEMBERS OF THE CHURCH

What the above discussion has attempted to indicate is that for a real reader to be able to assume the role of the implied reader of Matthew's Gospel, such a reader must regard himself or herself as a member of the believing community presupposed by Matthew's Gospel. This conclusion, resulting from the methodology of narrative criticism, is actually integral to the presuppositional framework of another methodology which developed independent of narrative criticism. Canonical criticism, the methodology to be discussed in the next chapter, stands or falls on the presupposition that the reader of the Gospel of Matthew or of any biblical book is a member of the believing community.

SUGGESTIONS FOR FURTHER READING

Anderson, J.C., "Matthew: Gender and Reading," *Semeia* 28 (1983) 3–27.

Jauss, H.R., "Levels of Identification of Hero and Audience," *New Literary History* 5 (1974) 283–317.

Edwards, R.A., *Matthew's Story of Jesus* (Philadelphia: Fortress, 1985).

Via, D.O., "Narrative World and Ethical Response: The Marvelous and Righteousness in Matthew 1–2," *Semeia* 12 (1978) 123–149.

Waetjen, H.C., "The Genealogy as the Key to the Gospel according to Matthew," *Journal of Biblical Literature* 95 (1976) 205–230.

Chapter 8

CANONICAL CRITICISM

Canonical criticism is in many ways the most recent type of criticism being applied to the Bible. The first significant work dealing with this methodology appeared in 1972 (James Sanders, *Torah and Canon*) but its presuppositions and methods can be found in the activity of believing communities from the earliest stages of the development of the Bible. Canonical criticism grew out of and can be seen as a development of the historical-critical method. Nevertheless it differs from the historical-critical method insofar as it is largely a synchronic approach which goes beyond the work of the final redactor and views the canonical text as a unity in the context of the believing community which reads, accepts and passes it on. Canonical criticism, therefore, shares with reader-response criticism and structuralism a recognition of the importance of the reader in interpreting the biblical text.

1. THE QUESTION OF THE CANON

The question of the canon of Scripture has long been discussed by biblical scholars. Since the fourth century A.D. the term "canon" has been used to refer to the authoritative list of books accepted as Holy Scripture. The question of the canon is therefore the question of which books and which form of these books belong in the Bible. The question is not as easy as it might seem. Catholic Bibles contain a number of books and parts of books which are not found in Protestant Bibles. In some Prot-

estant Bibles, e.g., the Oxford Annotated Bible, there are included, usually in the back in a section headed "The Apocrypha,"
the material that Catholics think belong in the Bible and Protestants do not. Even greater variations are found in some Orthodox and Coptic Christian Bibles.

Until recently the question of the canon was treated by historical-critical scholars in introductions. Before any critical study
of the Bible could begin one had to establish the text that one
would be studying. Usually all that one finds in historical-critical
works is a decision about which books belong in the Bible and a
brief explanation of the basis for that decision. The works then
get on with the business of analyzing the Bible without ever returning to the question of the canon.

Unfortunately the question of the canon cannot be handled
that easily. What really belongs in the Bible? How is or was the
decision made about what belongs in the Bible? Who decides
what belongs in the Bible? These are the questions that canonical
criticism considers to be of momentous importance. When the
questions are taken seriously the importance of the canon will
enter into the methodology being used to interpret the canonical
text.

2. TEXT AND COMMUNITY

In profane literary criticism, reader-response critics reacted
against the scientific objectivity of the New Critics. In biblical
studies canonical critics are reacting against historical criticism
on somewhat parallel grounds. Reader-response critics claim that
literary theorists, since the middle of the eighteenth century,
have been denying that literature possesses the ability to influence human behavior in a direct and practical way, an understanding of literature that dates back to the ancient Greek
rhetoricians. In the concluding chapter of her book, *Reader-Response Criticism,* Jane Tompkins explains how and why this modern development away from the ancient Greek understanding
occurred in profane literary studies. This development, she
maintains, is actually an outgrowth of the Enlightenment which
tended to place all studies on an objective foundation. Reader-

response criticism is reacting against this Enlightenment mentality by insisting that literature does directly influence human behavior. In effect what contemporary literary critics, i.e., reader-response critics, are doing is reacting against modern scientific positivism and returning to the view held by ancient Greek rhetoricians about what it was that literature does. Their methodology is quite new but their insistence on the involvement of the reader in determining the meaning of a text is really quite ancient.

In a similar way, canonical critics complain, as does Sanders in *Canon and Community*, that Enlightenment scholarship took the Bible away from the Church's lectern and put it in the scholar's study. Historical critics have discussed in detail the various situations in life (*Sitz im Leben*) which serve as the interpretive background for the books of the New Testament, i.e., the situation in the life of Jesus, the situation in the life of the early community and the situation in the life of the final author or redactor. For canonical critics the true *Sitz im Leben* of the Bible are the believing communities which are the heirs of those who formed and shaped it in antiquity. Historical critics, by focusing on the meaning of the text at pre-canonical levels have decanonized the text, rendering difficult its application to the contemporary religious scene. In their focus on the original historical meaning historical critics have maintained that the meaning of the text derives not from the community that accepts and canonizes it but exists apart from and independent of that community.

Structuralists emphasize the reader's situation and condition as being essential to understanding the text but what they emphasize is the universal structuring capacity that lies deep in the unconscious of every reader. Structuralists, however, maintain that a rigorous application of their methodology would yield a single objective meaning for the text. Canonical critics agree on the importance of the reader's situation and condition but move rather in the direction of reader-response criticism by holding that literature is multivalent, i.e., every work of literature has many meanings. Canonical critics agree with reader-response critics that it is the reader who produces the meaning of the text but insist as one of their fundamental presuppositions that it is only the believing community that is capable of reading and interpreting the Bible. This presupposition would seem to be confirmed by the analysis in Chapter VII of the reader of Matthew's Gospel, an analysis which used the methodology of reader-response criticism.

3. TEXT AND HISTORY

3.1 Text or History behind the Text

An extremely important contribution to canonical criticism was made in a work published in 1979 by Brevard Childs entitled *Introduction to the Old Testament as Scripture*. Childs was one of the ground-breakers in the contemporary development of canonical criticism. The title of his work is initially puzzling. Since the Old Testament is obviously Scripture, how else would one introduce it? The point that Childs is trying to make is that many works on the Old Testament do not treat it as Scripture.

A good illustration of the approach that Childs takes can be found in his treatment of the Books of Ezra and Nehemiah. These are very interesting books for the historical critic because, obviously, they are all messed up. There are very significant historical questions that cannot be answered by a straightforward reading of Ezra and Nehemiah. Who came first, Ezra or Nehemiah? Were they ever in Jerusalem at the same time? Did their careers overlap? Which was the Artaxerxes under whom Ezra came to Jerusalem? Did Ezra come in 458 B.C., or 428, or 398, or some other year? It is clear that the Books of Ezra and Nehemiah consist of pieces of literature that have been rearranged by subsequent redactors. The present form of these books disturbs the correct historical sequence of events. It is the work of historical critics to examine the traditions that lie behind the works of Ezra and Nehemiah, using all of the historical-critical tools at their disposal, to reconstruct what really happened in the missions of Ezra and Nehemiah. Such studies have yielded significant but disparate results. Historical critics are today no closer to a consensus on the problems surrounding Ezra and Nehemiah than they were decades ago.

The investigations of the historical critics are certainly legitimate, they are certainly interesting, but, according to Childs, such studies fail to appreciate the books of Ezra and Nehemiah precisely as Scripture. The fact of the matter is that in the canonical text the Books of Ezra and Nehemiah are arranged the way they are. That is the canonical text. What is the canonical text saying? Historical critics seem to be oblivious to this question. They try to see what is on the other side of the window without looking at the window itself, without recognizing that the canonical text is not merely something to be looked through but that it is meant to be looked at. That is where the real meaning of the text is to be found. If all one does is look at the other side of the text, then the whole point of the biblical book precisely as Scripture is missed. Childs entitled the book as he did because for him the Old Testament is Scripture and not merely a source book for the history that lies behind the Scripture.

What Childs does with the Books of Ezra and Nehemiah is that he takes the canonical text seriously. What does the text itself mean? Perhaps from the perspective of an historical critic, the way it is arranged does not make sense. Such, however, is of little concern to a member of the believing community that has accepted the text as canonical. What one should be interested in is the inspired text, the canonical text that was taken into the life of the believing community. What does this text mean? The canonized text, as it is, is where the meaning of Scripture is to be found.

Childs has recently applied the same approach to the New Testament in his book *The New Testament as Canon: An Introduction*. What is required in both Testaments is a synchronic approach to the text. What is important in the Gospels is not what may or may not have happened in the life of Jesus but the Gospel text itself, precisely what is studied by other synchronic exegetical methods such as structuralism. Whether or not historians are ever able to figure out the precise chronology of the events of Holy Week is of little importance. What is important are the four different chronological arrangements found in the actual texts of the four Gospels.

3.2 Text or History after the Text

In his earlier work on the Old Testament Childs had placed considerable emphasis on the moment of stabilization (e.g., the moment in time when the Book of Isaiah was redacted or edited for the final time into the form in which it now exists) as being decisive for the canonical shape of the text and therefore for its meaning as Scripture. More recently James Sanders, in *Canon and Community,* has placed much more emphasis on the process whereby a text becomes canonical. While the moment of stabilization is certainly significant, even more significant is the fact that these stabilized texts were repeated. The Books of Ezra and Nehemiah not only were composed the way they were, but they were repeated; they were handed on; they were copied.

The Gospel of Matthew was not only composed the way it was, but it was copied and handed on, and used, and eventually canonized. The Gospel of Matthew was not canonical the day it was written. The hypothetical source, Q, was not canonical the day it was written, and it was never canonical. Whatever it was, it eventually disappeared. Paul wrote all kinds of letters. No one knows how many. None of them were canonical the day they were written. Some of them, generations later or centuries later, became canonical.

What is eventually canonized is what belongs between the covers of the Bible. It is a process that takes generations, or even centuries. The process has already occurred but what was involved in that process is significant not only for how the Church once understood the Scriptures but also for how the Church continues to understand the Scriptures in every age.

Unfortunately the results of that process continue to be disputed among Christians of the present day. Canonical criticism can shed light on the question of the limits of the canon but it is primarily concerned with studying the canonical process itself as a basis for interpreting the biblical texts as we have them today.

4. DIACHRONIC AND SYNCHRONIC METHODOLOGY

The methodology of canonical criticism, while primarily synchronic, is also diachronic and related to the historical-critical method. It is diachronic insofar as it is concerned with a stage in the historical process through which the biblical texts moved. While form criticism is concerned with the activity of the believing community in selecting and shaping traditions and redaction criticism is concerned with the activity of the final editors or authors of the various books of the Bible, canonical criticism is concerned with the activity of the subsequent communities of faith which accepted these books as canonical.

Canonical criticism is synchronic and related to structuralism and reader-response criticism insofar as it recognizes that what is of greatest importance is the canonical text which has been handed on in believing communities. While canonical critics do study historical processes, they do not read the text historically. In his book on the New Testament, Childs opposes the position of historical critics who assume that the meaning of a text derives from a specific historical referent. For Childs, the canonical process had the precise function of loosening the text from any one historical setting.

5. CANONICAL PROCESS

Canonical criticism has two major foci, canonical process and canonical hermeneutics, the latter flowing from and depending upon the former. Canonical critics are primarily concerned with providing tools for reading the canonical text but they do so through understanding the canonical process in antiquity, the process by which certain texts in stable form were accepted as canonical by the believing community. Using an array of methods drawn from historical and literary criticism, canonical critics have been able to uncover some of the significant factors involved in this process.

5.1 Pluralism

The processes by which both the Hebrew canon of Scripture and the Christian canon were formed were marked by pluralism and fluidity. There was never a single orthodox perspective around which the canon was formed. There were, instead, a plurality of perspectives which existed and developed side by side. In the context of this pluralism the collections of sacred literature were subject, during the period of canonical processes, to constant fluctuation. During the first century A.D. the only books recognized as authoritative by all Jews were the five books of Moses, the Torah. The Pharisees used a much larger number of books and the Essenes used books not used by the Pharisees. Jews of the diaspora not only had diverse collections of books but used texts that differed significantly in order and content from those used in Palestine. The situation in the early centuries of Christianity was much the same. It was not until well into the fourth century A.D. that Christians came to use a somewhat fixed and universal canon.

Not only was there diversity in the lists of books used but there was also diversity in the content of these books. Marcion, a second century heretic, wanted the sacred literature of Christianity to speak with one voice, i.e., the voice of Luke and Paul. Believing communities rejected Marcion, preferring a multiple Gospel canon and an Old Testament even more diverse than the Hebrew canon that was gaining acceptance within post-temple Judaism.

5.2 Multivalence and Acceptance by the Church

A significant feature of canonical criticism is the recognition that texts are canonized only if they are flexible. If a text is too narrowly conceived, if it has meaning only in a specific, limited situation, a well-defined meaning for a specific point in time, it is not going to be repeated, it is not going to be taken up into the life of the Church. Something that is flexible in meaning, something that can be repeated again and again and speak to the changing life situations of the Church, is going to be taken up by the Church and utilized by the Church precisely because of its flexibility. Eventually it will be canonized by the Church because the Church will recognize that this text speaks to the life of the Church in every age.

An enormous volume of literature was written in the thousand year period during which time the books of the Bible were written, but only these books were canonized. Only these books are Scripture, because only these books were seen by the Church as speaking to the life of the Church in every age. What canonical critics see taking place in the life of the Church after the composition of the various books of the Bible is very similar to what form critics see taking place in the period before their composition. According to form critics traditions about the words and deeds of Jesus were handed on in a process that involved selection and adaptation according to the liturgical and instructional needs of the early Christian community. According to canonical critics a similar process occurred in the later Christian community once the various books had been composed. There was selection and repetition according to the liturgical and instructional needs of the Church. Those books that survived this process of selection and repetition are those books that the Church eventually canonized precisely because they served the needs of the Church.

5.3 Stabilization and Beyond

In the early Christian centuries the believing community was being shaped by the literature it inherited and used. At the same time it was shaping this literature. It was selecting and preserving those books that spoke to its life situation and putting these books into their final form. Most importantly it was rendering these books adaptable to its changing life situation by the hermeneutical technique of resignification.

What is of greatest importance for canonical critics, therefore, is not the original intent of the author or even of the final canonical redactor. It is not the understanding of the original audience nor even of the believing community which eventually accepted the book as canonical. Even after stabilization the same process of repetition and application within the believing community continues as the text serves the purposes and needs of successive communities. When the historical phenomenon occurs of the leaders and faithful of a believing community finding value for themselves in a given writing, then this writing has a life of its own, a life which continues to the present day. What is of greatest importance, therefore, is the role of the canonical text within the life of the present day believing community.

6. CANONICAL HERMENEUTICS

Recognizing the primacy of the canonical text over the history that preceded it and understanding the canonical process by which the text became part of the life of the believing community, one can then ask "What does it mean?" Canonical hermeneutics responds to this question but in a way quite different from methods that seek an objectively verifiable meaning in the text. Canonical hermeneutics emphasizes the richness of the canon and the plurality of meanings.

6.1 Hermeneutic Triangle

Like historical criticism, canonical criticism studies the historical processes leading to a text. It studies the traditions and sources that eventually become part of the canonical text, but it is most concerned with the manner in which this material functions in the canonical text, i.e., how this material is used and interpreted within the canonical text. With such a focus canonical criticism derives its own interpretive methodology from the interpretive methodology that can be discerned in and between the lines of the canonical text itself.

The canonical process involved many stages in which existing material was seen to be significant by a believing community and was therefore adapted and repeated by that community. The oracles of the prophet Isaiah were collected, arranged and written down. A later generation repeated this writing with substantial additions. Centuries later the Christian community repeated this expanded writing in the context of its own faith situation. Each stage of the canonical process can be analyzed in terms of the triangle illustrated in figure 8.1. The three angles of this triangle represent the three factors that are always involved in the canonical process whether it is at the pre-textual stage when traditions were being used and collected, at the post-textual stage when the early communities of faith accepted certain texts as can-

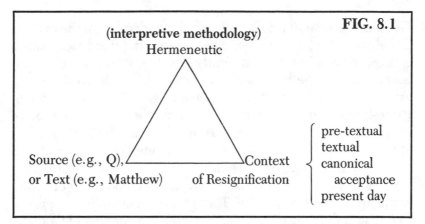

FIG. 8.1

(interpretive methodology)
Hermeneutic

Source (e.g., Q), — Context
or Text (e.g., Matthew)   of Resignification

⎧ pre-textual
⎪ textual
⎨ canonical
⎪   acceptance
⎩ present day

onical, or in the present day when believing communities read and use these texts.

Canonical critics use the tools of historical criticism to analyze the source that is being used, e.g., the hypothetical source "Q" that was used by the authors of Matthew and Luke. They use these tools as well to understand the context in which the source is being used and resignified. They are especially interested in the situation, the sociological context, of the believing communities that found value in these sources and moved them along the path of the canonical process. What is most important, however, is the top angle of the triangle that unites source and context, the hermeneutics by which the sources or texts function in the contexts of communities both past and present. This is the unrecorded hermeneutics that lies in and between the lines of the canonical text.

6.2 Theocentric Hermeneutic

Canonical critics emphasize the plurality of meanings that can be found in a biblical text but they do not advocate rampant subjectivism. It is possible, by applying the appropriate interpretive technique, to make a biblical text say whatever one wants it to say. Canonical criticism, however, insists that its hermeneutics flow from the hermeneutics that can be discerned along the various stages of the canonical process.

Historical critics have long recognized that the flood story in

Genesis 6–9 is similar to and clearly dependent upon the ancient Babylonian Gilgamesh epic. The pre-existing flood story was a source, but a believing community took that story and adapted it according to some hermeneutical principle for its own life situation. If one compares the canonical text of Genesis to the Gil-gamesh epic, one sees that the differences are even more profound than the similarities. In the Gilgamesh epic there is a story about a man, Utnapishtim, who rides out the flood and earns immortality by his obedience and good deeds. Utnapishtim's counterpart in the Genesis story, Noah, ends up mortal and sinful just like everyone else. The story in Genesis, however, unlike that in the Gilgamesh epic, stresses the oneness of God and his ethical integrity. The Genesis story is actually more about God than it is about Noah.

What canonical critics discern in the Genesis story is a theocentric hermeneutic by means of which pre-existing material was adapted for the needs of a believing community. James Sanders believes that this same theocentric hermeneutic pervades the entirety of the canon. It is a hermeneutic that governed the shaping of the canon and a hermeneutic that should govern its interpretation today.

6.3 Resignification

When believing communities take up existing material into their lives of faith there is always a certain amount of resignification. An example of this process can be seen in the use of the term "Zion" in the Book of Isaiah. It is generally recognized that only the earlier part of the book (most of Chapters 1 to 39) pertain to the life and preaching of the historical Isaiah. The remainder of the book was composed after the exile. What is important for canonical criticism is not what the prophet Isaiah intended nor even what various others who had a hand in the book intended but rather how the unified book functioned in the believing community.

Reading the unified text one can discern the interpretive process at work in that text. The term "Zion" had one signification in the life and ministry of Isaiah. If one reads Isaiah 31:4f in the light of that historical ministry, it is clear that Zion is a political entity which the Lord will protect from its enemies.

> The Lord of hosts will come down to fight upon Mount Zion and upon its hill. Like birds hovering, so the Lord of hosts will protect Jerusalem; he will protect and deliver it, he will spare and rescue it (Is 31:4f).

If, on the other hand, one reads Isaiah 60:2f in the context of the book as a whole, one sees that in the canonical text Zion has been resignified. Zion is no longer a political entity being spared from its enemies but rather it is the place to which all peoples will come to learn God's law. This resignification is part of the canonical text's perception of the real identity of Israel as God's teacher for all creation.

> For behold, darkness shall cover the earth, and thick darkness the peoples; but the Lord will arise upon you and his glory will be seen upon you. And nations shall come to your light, and kings to the brightness of your rising (Is 60:2f).

By studying the manner and range of resignification that takes place within the biblical texts, canonical critics hope to provide guidelines for the interpretive process today. Canonical critics are interested in what the prophet Isaiah intended. They are also interested in what the believing community had in mind when the text of Isaiah was stabilized. They derive their hermeneutic, however, from the hermeneutic at work in the canonical process itself.

A certain amount of resignification takes place every time a passage is read. Preachers and teachers have been resignifying biblical texts from earliest days. Unlike many historical critics who deplore what they consider to be abuses of Scripture, i.e., departures from the original meaning of the text, canonical critics hope to be more responsive to the needs and traditional practices of the believing communities.

SUGGESTIONS FOR FURTHER READING

Ackroyd, P., "Original Text and Canonical Text," *Union Seminary Quarterly Review* 32 (1977) 166–173.

Barton, J., *Reading the Old Testament: Method in Biblical Study* (Philadelphia: Fortress, 1984).

Brueggemann, W., *The Creative Word: Canon as a Model for Biblical Education* (Philadelphia: Fortress, 1982).

Childs, B., *The Book of Exodus: A Critical Theological Commentary* (Philadelphia: Fortress, 1974).

Childs, B., *Introduction to the Old Testament as Scripture* (Philadelphia: Fortress, 1979).

Childs, B., *The New Testament as Canon: An Introduction* (Philadelphia: Fortress, 1985).

Coats, G.W., and B.O. Long (eds.), *Canon and Authority: Essays in Old Testament Religion and Theology* (Philadelphia: Fortress, 1977).

Lemcio, E., "The Gospels and Canonical Criticism," *Biblical Theology Bulletin* 11 (1981) 114–122.

Sanders, J.A., *Canon and Community* (Philadelphia: Fortress, 1984).

Sanders, J.A., "Canonical Context and Canonical Criticism," *Horizons in Biblical Theology* 2 (1980) 173–197.

Sanders, J.A., "Text and Canon: Concepts and Methods," *Journal of Biblical Literature* 98 (1979) 5–29.

Chapter 9

THE BIBLE IN THE CHURCH TODAY

The new methodologies discussed in the preceding chapters could have a profound effect on the relationship between the Church and the Scriptures. In this chapter some of the implications of these new methodologies will be discussed.

1. THE BIBLE AS THE CHURCH'S BOOK

Canonical critics have emphasized the fact that the Bible is primarily the Church's book and that such was the common understanding of Scripture from the earliest centuries. James Sanders has observed that Enlightenment scholarship took the Scriptures out of the Church's lectern and placed them in the scholars' study. This alteration of the ancient relationship between the Church and Scripture was actually rooted in an earlier development, the Reformation. As discussed in Chapter II, the Reformation itself significantly affected the relationship between Church and Scripture. At the time of the Reformation the Bible became a weapon to be used against the Church; in fact it was the primary weapon used against the Church. The reformers' understanding of the Bible differed radically from the understanding of the Bible as the Church's book, the Bible which is canonized by the Church, taken up into the life of the Church precisely because it is seen as serving the Church. The reformers, in the interest of reform, were actually driving a wedge between the Bible and the Church.

The Reformation churches desperately needed the Bible for solidity, for stability, because the Bible was all they had. They had eliminated or significantly curtailed the effectiveness and meaningfulness of the hierarchical, sacramental Church. They had the Bible, but they needed a Bible that could provide a reliable and firm foundation for their faith and life. The subsequent development at the time of the Enlightenment is not hard to understand. It was easy, if not almost necessary, to entrust the Bible to the scholars' study where the methods of Enlightenment scholarship could be used to make of the Bible something solid and objective on which Reformation Christianity could stand.

Reformed Christianity needed objective, historical biblical scholarship. Sanders has observed that today virtually all Protestants, whether they are liberal or conservative, view the Bible in a way that accords to it an existence separate from the faith of the community. The believing community is bracketed out in biblical scholarship, whether it be conservative or liberal Protestant scholarship. Even Catholics who follow the historical-critical method have done basically the same thing. They have bracketed out the believing community in applying their critical methodology to the study of the Bible. Recent methodologies like reader-response criticism, which emphasize the role of the reader in biblical interpretation, and especially canonical criticism, which sees the believing community as the proper reader of the Bible, offer scholars a means of restoring the ancient relationship between Bible and Church, of viewing the Bible as the Church's book.

2. THE CHURCH AS READER AND CANONIZER

The separation between the critical interpretation of the Bible and the faith of the community was nowhere to be found in the Church in the early centuries. It was scarcely to be found anywhere in Christianity all the way up to the Reformation. The insights that biblical studies are today borrowing from reader-response criticism seem to suggest that this separation needs to be overcome. What reader-response critics today maintain is that the activity of reading is a social activity. Private interpretation, the work of autonomous individuals who read a work and understand it by themselves, is an impossibility even for those who think they are doing it. All readers come to a book, any book, with convictions, with beliefs, with concerns, with values that arise out of a social atmosphere. To pretend that one can bracket out the societal aspect in the reading process is to be deceived. It cannot be done when one reads Shakespeare, it cannot be done when one reads Matthew. Everyone is part of a believing community, and the faith of that community is part of the reading process. Furthermore, one who does not participate in the faith community that is presupposed of the implied reader of a given text simply cannot read that text.

The implied reader of Matthew's Gospel, discussed in Chapter VII, reads that Gospel as a member of the Christian community. Apart from being a member of the Christian community, one cannot accept the role required of the implied reader of the text, i.e., one simply cannot read the Gospel of Matthew. One can analyze it as a scientist, but one cannot read it and receive from it its intended effect.

There is, in fact, something to be said for the opinion of some historical critics that the disciples of Matthew's Gospel represent the Church of Matthew's day. Narrative critics would caution against committing the referential fallacy but their methodology does lead to the conclusion that the reader is, on the one hand, encouraged by the text to identify with the disciples and, on the other hand, that the reader must be part of the social community, the Church, in order to fulfill the role demanded by the text of the implied reader. While the specific assertion that the disciples represent the Church is probably erroneous, the fact remains that scholars were able to use this insight to draw conclusions about Matthew's Gospel. The historical critics who advanced this theory, however, would probably not be willing to accept the full implications of the insight that the proper reader of Matthew is the Church, not the Church of Matthew's day but the Church of any day.

One of the greatest concerns which historical critics express when evaluating reader-response criticism is a concern for some guarantee of objectivity. It should be observed, however, that much of the concern about objectivity is rooted in the Reformation/Enlightenment separation of Scripture from the Church. When Scripture is separated from the Church and compelled somehow to stand on its own, then there is a need for some kind of a critical method that will give to Scripture an objective meaning. If Scripture is the Church's book, if Scripture is canonized precisely because it is seen as speaking to the Church, as coming forth from the Church, then the needed guarantee of objectivity is to be found in the Church. The reliability of the Church is far more important than an objectively verifiable critical methodology.

The methodology of reader-response criticism leads one to recognize that the reader implied by the text of the Bible is a believing Christian, a member of the Church. The position of canonical critics, though arising from a different perspective, is much the same. For them the reader of the Bible is the Church. The two methodologies seem to converge at this point; the importance of the believing community or the Church, and the insights of reader-response criticism can be used to understand and explain the position of canonical criticism.

According to canonical critics, there was a period of intense canonical process in the early centuries of the Church during which time certain books were selected, repeated and adapted. By the end of this period, certainly by some time in the fourth century, there was a rather well defined list of books, henceforth referred to as the canon, which the Church accepted as authoritative. There is no indication that there was, in the early part of this period, any *a priori* criterion that was used to determine which books should be selected and canonized. The process simply happened in the course of the life of the Church. It was only at a later date that an attempt was made to assign a criterion, e.g., apostolicity, for the process that had already occurred.

One may still, however, raise the question of why some of the books that were written were canonized and others were not. To respond in the language of reader-response criticism, one could say that the Church saw itself as the implied reader of certain books and made them a part of its life. With other books, the Gospel of Thomas, Q, and many other things that were written, the Church did not see itself as the implied reader. The Church saw the implied reader of these books as something at odds with itself, or something at least not fully identified with itself, and thus did not canonize them.

3. WHICH BOOKS BELONG IN THE BIBLE?

Which books did the Church canonize? The problem of the different lists of canonical books found in Catholic, Protestant and other Christian Bibles still needs to be resolved. Brevard Childs, in his *Introduction to the Old Testament as Scripture*, defended the traditional Protestant list of Old Testament books. He did so by focusing on the moment of stabilization of the canonical literature of Pharisaic Judaism. James Sanders, also a Protestant, has taken issue with Childs' narrow definition of the canon. With a more thoroughgoing application of the methodology of canonical criticism Sanders emphasizes the fluidity of the canon throughout the period of intense canonical process. He therefore, unlike Childs, rejects the attempt of the Protestant reformers to narrow the Old Testament canon (*Canon and Community*, p. 35).

Historically, at the time of the Reformation, the Bible was made to stand on its own, and eventually made to stand on some kind of historical foundation apart from the Church. For the Bible to be able to criticize the Church it had to stand on its own apart from the Church. It was therefore necessary to have a basis for determining the canon apart from the Church. The criterion of apostolicity served as a basis for the New Testament canon, but what criterion independent of the Church could be used for the Old Testament canon? The answer was obvious—the Jewish canon. It was decided to accept as canonical Old Testament books those books that Judaism considered to be canonical. As a result the Protestant Old Testament has the same books as the Jewish Old Testament.

This decision on the part of the reformers was not without precedent. Though Western Christianity generally accepted what is now the Catholic Old Testament as canonical from at least the fourth century onward, there were a number of significant conflicting voices. The most noteworthy of these voices was that of St. Jerome, the fourth century translator of the Latin version of the Bible known as the Vulgate. Jerome set about to translate the Bible into Latin from the original languages. He was surprised when he found that the Hebrew Bible did not contain all of the books currently being used in Christian Bibles. While he included these additional books in his Bible he relegated them to a lesser status and held that they should not be used to establish ecclesiastical dogmas. Other voices in the fourth century, however, were stronger and clearer, including St. Augustine, the Bishop of Hippo, and a number of ecclesiastical synods. All of these unanimously declared the longer list of the books of the Christian Old Testament to be canonical.

At the time of the Reformation the reformers chose to follow Jerome rather than Augustine and over a thousand years of ecclesiastical tradition. Two factors, both related to the Reformation concern that the Scriptures have an authority independent of the Church, probably influenced their decision in favor of the Hebrew canon. First, their desire for something solid which preexisted the Church led them to the texts in the original languages. Like Jerome they found the shorter Old Testament canon in the Hebrew Bible. Second, their use of the Scriptures as a basis for arguing against the Church led them to seek some basis for their canon other than decisions of Church synods. The existing canon of the Hebrew Bible satisfied this need.

The acceptance of the Hebrew canon is, however, problematic in a number of ways. The most obvious difficulty lies in the fact that the reformers based their criterion for the Old Testament canon not on Christianity but on Judaism. This basis would seem to presume that the believing community of Jews could choose those books in which the Christian community would see itself as the implied reader. It could be protested that Christianity comes out of Judaism and originally accepted as its own those books which Judaism had already accepted as its own. Such, however, historically was not the case. Recent historical studies have shown that in a certain sense the Jewish Old Testament is later than the Christian Old Testament. The reformers probably thought that the Jewish Old Testament, being Jewish, must have preceded the Christian Old Testament and that Christians had added a number of books to this Jewish Old Testament to come up with the Old Testament that is found in the Septuagint and the Catholic Bibles. The reformers, wanting to get back to something solid that was prior to and not dependent on the Church, excluded these additional books.

In point of fact, however, there was no canonical Old Testament among the Jews prior to Christianity. There was the law (the Pentateuch, the Torah) that all Jews and Samaritans recognized as the foundation of their religion. There were also the prophets, which were accorded considerable authority by many but not all Jews. Then there were a wide assortment of other writings that were used in varying degrees by Jews in various parts of the world. Christianity does indeed find its roots in Judaism, but it was Christians themselves who, during the first century of Christianity, chose to use that array of Jewish books that would later be found in the Septuagint and in Catholic Bibles. The first century Christians accepted them because they saw themselves as the implied readers of these books. This is precisely what is involved in that passage from 2 Corinthians 3:15 that was discussed in Chapter VI. The Jews, when they read Moses, read it with a veil over their eyes. Christians, however, can read Moses. Why? Because the veil has been removed by the Spirit that makes them able to read what the Spirit wants them to read in these books. What developed among Christians in the first century, beginning around the time of Paul, was an aware- ness that a whole array of Jewish literature was their literature; it was speaking to them, speaking to their life situation. Regard- less of their varying degrees of acceptance among Jews, these books had meaning for Christians and ultimately were canonized. These are the books that eventually became the Septuagint, the Greek Old Testament used by the Christians.

A further consideration that is important for appreciating the relationship between the Jewish and Christian Old Testament canons is the fact that the technology for binding books was only discovered around the end of the first century A.D. Prior to this discovery each book was on a separate scroll, and the question of which books should be bound together into a Bible had never been asked. When eventually the question was asked, it was a question without precedent, and, as the discussions about both the Old and New Testaments throughout the second and third centuries show, it was a long time before the Church gave a definitive answer. When an answer was given, however, it was based on the consistent practice of the Church from earliest times. From earliest times the Christian community had appropriated as its own a larger group of Old Testament writings than eventually were to be found in the Hebrew Bible.

A parallel but independent development occurred in Judaism. After the destruction of the temple in Jerusalem and after the formation of the synagogue at Jamnia, the center of later rabbinic Judaism, the Jews gradually decided on their own list. They decided that many of the books that the Christians were using, and that some Jews formerly had used, really did not speak to the new self-understanding of post-temple rabbinic Judaism. The new self-understanding was no longer attuned to books like Maccabees that seemed to encourage the kind of militaristic apocalyptic that had brought on the destruction of the temple. These later Jews eventually came up with a shorter Old Testament canon which excluded many of the books that Christians were already using.

This selection of books made by the Jews is really unimportant for a Christian consideration of the canon of Scripture. What is canonical is what the Church accepted. Canonical critics today are recognizing the error that the reformers made in accepting the Hebrew canon, but that error was based on and almost necessitated by the initial cleavage that the reformers had drawn between Scripture and the Church.

4. THE CHURCH AND INSPIRATION

Christians of all times have been virtually unanimous in maintaining that the Bible is inspired. On the question of what precisely is meant by inspiration, however, there is no such unanimity. There are actually two separate matters that are often confused, inspiration itself and the effects of inspiration. The more commonly discussed question is the secondary question about the effects of inspiration which for many Christians involves some kind of authority and inerrancy. The most bitter disputes arise over the question of inerrancy, with many fundamentalists insisting on almost propositional infallibility and most critical scholars interpreting inerrancy in terms of their particular methodology. An historical critic, for example, would insist on being allowed to sort through the various levels of development and find different kinds of truth at each level. Some things are historically true, others are true expressions of the preaching, teaching and worshiping needs of the early Christian community, while still others are true expressions of the theology of the final redactor. The discussion about the nature of inspiration itself, which will occupy most of the remainder of this chapter, should provide a perspective for appreciating the secondary question of inerrancy.

4.1 Inspiration Itself

When one speaks of the books of the Bible as inspired, what is usually meant is that though they were clearly written by humans they are unlike all other human literature because God is, in some unique way, involved in their production. The primary question about inspiration concerns precisely how God is involved in the production of the books of the Bible. Does God so overpower the human author that all human originality or creativity is eliminated? Does God allow a measure of creativity, and if so, how much? Can the human author make mistakes in trivial matters or even in more important matters? The most basic question, however, concerns where inspiration is to be located. Is it to be located in the author of the text, in the text itself or perhaps even in the reading of the text?

Canonical criticism and reader-response criticism have been presented in this book as new methodologies that hold great promise for the future of biblical studies in the Church. One of the reasons they hold such promise is that together they can be used to offer a reasonable and satisfactory explanation for the question of inspiration. Reader-response critics maintain that the text is a virtual entity that comes into being in the act of reading when the aesthetic pole, the reader, actualizes the artistic pole, the literary text. If the Bible, a literary work, is inspired its inspiration must be located at both poles. This suggestion is quite similar to the contention by James Sanders that "the Word of God

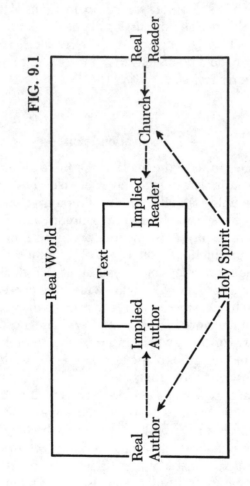

FIG. 9.1

happens or takes place at the nexus of text and context." For Sanders, who emphasized the role of the believing community in reading and interpreting the Scriptures, the canonical text becomes the word of God over and over again as situations change and as the Holy Spirit wills (*Canon and Community*, p. 78).

Figure 9.1 is a modified version of figure 6.2 in Chapter VI which showed the relationship between the implied author and the implied reader in the textual framework of a literary work. The diagram of figure 9.1 includes as well two additional items, the Church and the Holy Spirit. The implied author, as discussed in Chapter VI, is that set of values, concerns and beliefs that the real author puts into the work. In the case of inspired literature what a real author creates is influenced by the Holy Spirit. The implied author that one discerns in a biblical book is, therefore, the inspired author. In a similar way the implied reader of a biblical book is the inspired reader. The implied reader, as discussed in Chapter VI, is the reader who can actualize the text by entering into the text, by accepting the pre-conditions of the text, its faith, its value system, its concerns. The implied reader of the biblical books is the Church which canonized the books in which it recognized itself as the implied reader, i.e., those books which have the Church, its faith, its value systems and its concerns as that set of beliefs, values and concerns that are defined by the text as the necessary pre-condition for reading the text. These pre-conditions are in the text because they are put there by the implied author (inspired author) and are required of the implied reader (the Church, the inspired reader). Those books whose implied reader the Church saw as identified with itself are those books that came to be by the inspiration of the Holy Spirit, the same Spirit by which the Church lives and believes.

4.2 Islam and the Reformation

The above explanation of inspiration is somewhat at odds with the contemporary, popular understanding of inspiration but it is much more in harmony with the traditional, pre-modern understanding. At least from the time of the Reformation, if not even before then, and up to the present day, Christianity has been plagued with what is fundamentally an Islamic view of inspiration. According to Islam, the Koran was written on the prophet's heart. That divine writing, for Islam, was how the inspiration of the Koran took place. According to Islam, the prophet Mohammed had some kind of a mystical experience in which the angel Gabriel revealed to him that God's word was inscribed on his heart. He was then commanded to recite the word of God that had been inscribed on his heart. Literally, what the word "Koran" means is "the recitation." What Mohammed did was that he merely recited the word of God that had been inscribed on his heart. His recitation was written down by others (Mohammed could neither read nor write), then Islam came forth from this inspired word.

According to Islam, then, the inspiration of the Koran is something that comes directly from God. It is an almost magical kind of thing that comes from God and onto paper with minimal, almost non-existent interference from any human agency. Mohammed is not the author in any sense of that word. With the Koran understood as this direct divine gift to man, it is easy to appreciate how it could be accepted as the foundation document that pre-existed the religion of Islam.

There is a similarity between this Islamic understanding of inspiration and certain instances of Old Testament prophetic inspiration. The words which the prophet Jeremiah speaks were put into his mouth by God himself (Jer 1:9; 2:1). Later Jeremiah is ordered to write down words that God had dictated to him (Jer 36:1–4, 32). Even closer to the Islamic model is the story of Ezekiel eating the scroll with the message he was to speak (Ez 2:9–3:3). Unlike Jeremiah who always remained in full possession of his power of reasoning, understood the messages communicated and actually entered into dialogue with God (Jer 20:7–18), Ezekiel neither understands the message nor is in full possession of his powers of reasoning.

There were some attempts within ancient and medieval Christianity to explain the inspiration of all the books of the Bible on the basis of this prophetic model, but this explanation was never the dominant one. In the medieval Church the most popular explanation was that based on the Aristotelian concept of instrumental causality. According to this explanation, the human author of each of the books remained in full possession of all human powers and functioned in a fully human fashion in composing the book. At the same time, however, God was using this human writer as his instrument and thereby produced a result which, while fully human, was also precisely what God intended it to be. It was not until the late seventeenth century that the notion of verbal dictation became the dominant explanation of inspiration within Protestant orthodoxy. According to this explanation the Holy Spirit dictated the very words of Scripture to the authors of the various books.

It is this later Protestant view of inspiration that bears a remarkable similarity to the Islamic understanding, though whether or not it was directly influenced by Islam is not clear. Not only do both views maintain direct divine responsibility for the very words of the text and minimize or eliminate human creativity, but both, as well, see the resulting document as the foundation document of their religions. The understanding of inspiration as verbal dictation that developed within Protestant orthodoxy supported the Reformation position that accorded to the Scriptures an existence independent of the Church. It therefore became possible to view the Bible as Islam viewed the Koran, as a foundation document.

The Bible, in this understanding, is the word of God, the almost magical word of God, that somehow gets from God onto paper with a minimum of human interference. Furthermore, and this is the most significant point, the Bible in some way pre-exists the Church. It is for this reason, a reason based on a rather Islamic view of inspiration, that many insist that if something cannot be found in Scripture then it does not belong in the Church. There is nothing about the Pope in Scripture. Reformed Christianity, therefore, has no need for a Pope. There is nothing about the seven sacraments in the Scriptures. Baptism and the Eucharist can be found but not holy orders or matrimony or the rest of the sacraments. Most Protestants, therefore, find some place for baptism and the Eucharist but eliminate the other five. Many Catholics, on the other hand, strain at finding hints of the remaining five sacraments, likewise manifesting their belief that Scripture is the foundation document of the Church, that it is the verbally inspired word of God that lies at the basis of the Church.

4.3 Canonical Criticism and the Analogies of Inspiration

A thoroughly Christian understanding of Scripture, of inspiration and of the relationship between Scripture and the Church needs to take into account what actually happened in the first century of Christianity. After the death and resurrection of Jesus the Christian community came into being. The living, vibrant, preaching, teaching, worshiping Christian community existed long before there was such a thing as the Bible. Before any of the books of the New Testament were written, before any of the books of the Old Testament were canonized, there was the Church. The Church came first. It was the Church, understanding itself, that later saw itself as the implied reader of this whole array of works, a whole array of Old Testament works, and, through the next century or two, a whole array of New Testament works. It was the Church that saw the Spirit by which it lives as the Spirit which is involved in the implied author of these works. Precisely because the same Spirit by which the Church lives is the Spirit by which these books live, the Church saw itself as the implied reader of these books and took these books into its life. It accepted these books and canonized these books. These books have meaning and validity in the life of the Church because the Church accepts them, because the Church canonizes them. Apart from the Church they would have had no meaning, no existence, no autonomy.

A generation ago the Thomistic biblical scholar Pierre Benoit offered an explanation of inspiration rooted in ancient and medieval understandings. According to Benoit, inspiration must be understood analogically, i.e., there are variations and degrees of inspiration. The Holy Spirit is involved in producing the total effect of Scripture and influences each participant in this total effect in the manner and degree necessary. Each of the human powers of the principal author of a book participates in the charism of inspiration but each participates analogically so that it is moved according to its nature and in proportion to its role in the total effect. Similarly all those who contributed, at various stages of development, to the production of the books were inspired, but in proportion to the nature of their contribution. In like manner Benoit applies this analogical concept of inspiration to the continuing activity of the Church in its use of the Scriptures for its life and faith.

The explanation of Benoit accords well with the direction in which recent canonical critics are moving. The methodology of canonical criticism is based on the assumption that the Holy Spirit is active all along the path of the canonical process: from the original words or events, through what was heard, understood and passed on in ancient believing communities, to how successive editors reshaped oral and written records, to the acceptance by the Church of finished texts on down to modern hearings and understandings of these texts. Figure 9.1, used earlier in this chapter to illustrate an understanding of inspiration based on reader-response criticism, illustrates as well the position of Benoit and of contemporary canonical critics, i.e., that the Holy Spirit is active at every stage that contributes to the total meaning effect of the Bible. According to James Sanders, canonical critics are only saying what the great theologians of the Church have always insisted on, namely that "the Bible can be Word of God only as read or heard by living persons in communities of faith" (*Canon and Community*, p. xvii).

4.4 Inspiration and the Incarnation

An idea that is fundamental for understanding what Christianity is all about is the idea of the incarnation, the idea of God entering into human flesh, of God becoming man. The idea is, if analyzed logically, absurd. It is impossible to conceptualize it. How could God become man? The Gospel of Matthew provides a way for dealing with the incarnation by presenting the story of Jesus' birth in terms of Joseph, the chaste spouse, who functions at the mythical level as the mediator between God and man. One cannot understand the incarnation but by means of myth one can cope with it. The incarnation is a mystery that either must be handled by some method other than logical objectivity or else it must be rejected.

Islam rejected the incarnation. This is one of its fundamental characteristics. Moslems consider themselves to be true monotheists. If one says that God becomes man, if one says that there are two or three persons in God, one is, according to Islam, deviating from pure monotheism. One is demeaning Allah, the one God. For Islam there is one God, and Mohammed is his prophet. The channel by which the one God entered into human reality was by inscribing his word upon the heart of Mohammed, who then recited it and had the recitation written down in the Koran. This Islamic mode of verbal inspiration leaves the one God up there, infinitely above the human community. That is, for Islam, pure monotheism.

Christianity, from an Islamic perspective, messes things up with the incarnation, the Trinity and all of the other things that intermingle the one, transcendent God with creaturely materiality, things like the sacraments, the Pope, the bishops and the councils. Islam eliminates all of this in order to have pure monotheism. The Islamic conception of God is much neater, much cleaner, and much easier to deal with.

Iconoclasm, which manifested itself within Christianity, was expressing basically the same concerns as Islam. It involved a rejection of the full implications of the incarnation. One should not have art. One should not draw pictures of God. One should not have statues or paintings of any kind that might suggest that anything material might be worthy of veneration. For the iconoclasts, God cannot be encompassed in materiality. Somehow God needed to be purified to allow him to be God. Iconoclasts did not reject the incarnation as such; they merely rejected an aspect of the incarnation, its manifestation in the worshiping life of the Church.

At the time of the Reformation there was a similar rejection of manifestations of the incarnation. The Reformation rejection was far less conscious and sudden than was that of Islam or the iconoclasts, but its effects were, nevertheless, serious. As Protestantism developed from Luther, Calvin, and on through the various other manifestations, it eventually yielded Unitarianism as its logical, progressive outcome. Unitarianism involves an explicit rejection of the incarnation. Theologically, the Unitarians are very similar to Moslems. Their basic tenet is that there is one God. That is why they are called Unitarians, not Trinitarians. In a Unitarian church there are no stained glass windows, no paintings, no statues, no crucifixes, just as in a mosque. Unitarianism comes at the end of a sequence, beginning with the reformers, that involves the progressive denial of implications of the incarnation and eventually of the incarnation itself.

A book by Leo Steinberg, mentioned in Chapter I, *The Sexuality of Christ in Renaissance Art and in Modern Oblivion*, asks the question, "Why does post-Renaissance art cover up the genitals of Christ?" Steinberg suggests that nudity and genital disclosure were esthetic strategies by which Christian artists expressed the humanity of the incarnate God and that sometime after the Renaissance Christians lost their appreciation of the full dimensions of the incarnation. Steinberg does not attribute this development to the reformers but it is probably more than just a coincidence that at the same time that artists stopped depicting the genitals of Christ, the reformers were removing images from their churches, reducing the number of the sacraments and rejecting an incarnational understanding of the hierarchy.

The inspired word of God, the Bible, is one manifestation of the incarnation that the reformers sought to preserve. However, when one separates this one manifestation from all of the other manifestations, e.g., sacraments and hierarchy, one is left with what is basically an Islamic view of inspiration. To appreciate what the Bible is in the context of the life of the Church, one must first see the Church for what it is. The Church is the continuation of the incarnation. The hierarchical Church, the sacramental Church, the preaching, believing, worshiping Church is the present day continuation of the incarnation. It lives by the Spirit of God, the Spirit which is Jesus' Spirit, the Spirit of the Church. The Spirit which makes the real author of the various books of the Bible to be the implied author of the inspired literature of Christianity is the Spirit of the Church. The Bible is the Church's book, a book that has meaning when it is read in the context of the faith of the Church. Apart from being read within the Church, it cannot be read. It can be examined by a scientist under a microscope, but it cannot be read in the sense of the implied reader being able to actualize it in a way that deepens faith, for outside of the Church it is not inspired.

5. SCHOLARS AND THE CHURCH

Historical-critical scholars could feel quite comfortable being called upon to help the Church understand what the Scriptures meant, for they had a scientifically verifiable method of analysis. Many of these same scholars are quite uncomfortable with methods like reader-response criticism which lack the possibility of objective verification. However, if those using the method of reader-response criticism accept the insights of canonical criticism the danger will be obviated. With the more ancient relationship between Church and scholarship restored, scholars will no longer find themselves in the awesome role of having the responsibility for determining the meaning the Church is to find in the Scriptures. Rather scholars will function more properly like music critics or drama critics whose roles are entirely subordinated to those who actually enjoy these art forms. Biblical critics will serve the Church which reads and appreciates the Scriptures. They can help the Church appreciate how and why the Scriptures function as they do, they can help the Church appreciate better the meaning which is found in the Scriptures, but it will be the living, vibrant, believing, Spirit-filled Church that uncovers this meaning, not scholars using objectively verifiable methods.

To say that the believing, Spirit-filled Church reads and interprets the Scriptures might express a kind of an ideal, but it is far from the real situation. In the real world the Church is composed of both saints and sinners, learned and ignorant at every level from the episcopacy to the laity. In the past the Scriptures have been seriously abused by members of the hierarchy as well as the laity. In the care of critical scholars the Scriptures have been rescued from most of these abuses. What guarantee is there if scholars relinquish their interpretive control over the Scriptures that these abuses will not return? Unfortunately there is no guarantee.

The alternative, however, is even less fortunate. The reaction among many contemporary scholars against the historical-critical method has been based not on its inability to provide clear and certain conclusions but rather on the limited scope of the conclusions it has been able to reach. Canonical criticism calls on the Church to rely on the guidance of the Spirit in probing the rich expanse of meaning to be found in the Scriptures. Reader-response criticism offers the Church a more satisfactory method for appreciating how and why the Scriptures have the effect they do have in the life of the Church.

An interesting illustration from the distant past involves the Christological disputes leading up to the conciliar declarations of the third and fourth centuries. Who is Jesus? How should the Church express its faith in Jesus? With some approaching the Scriptures literally, others allegorically, still others perhaps haphazardly, a wide variety of conflicting answers were given to these questions. Nevertheless, even using the rigorous procedures of the historical-critical method one would have to admit that there was some solid biblical basis for practically all of the Christological "isms" of the first four centuries. Narrative critics would suggest that most of these "isms" resulted from committing the referential fallacy, i.e., assuming that the Adoptionist Jesus of one passage or the Arian Jesus of another or the Docetist Jesus of still another referred to the real Jesus of the Church's faith rather than to the Jesus of the story world of the particular book. Canonical critics would maintain that what is really important is the effect that all of these stories had on the Church reading and understanding them by the light of the Holy Spirit. This total effect is what, in fact, resulted in the conciliar decrees, decrees that could never have resulted from the rigorous application of the objectively verifiable but very limited historical-critical method.

SUGGESTIONS FOR FURTHER READING

Achtemeier, P., *The Inspiration of Scripture* (Philadelphia: Westminster, 1980).

Benoit, P., *Aspects of Biblical Inspiration* (Chicago: Priory, 1965).

Betz, H.D. (ed.), *The Bible as a Document of the University* (Chico: Scholars, 1981).

Bird, P.A., *The Bible as the Church's Book* (Philadelphia: Westminster, 1982).

Campenhausen, H. von, *The Formation of the Christian Bible* (Philadelphia: Fortress, 1972).

Dulles, A., "Scripture: Recent Protestant and Catholic Views," *Theology Today* 37 (1980) 7–26.

Farmer, W., and D. Farkasfalvy, *The Formation of the New Testament Canon* (New York: Paulist, 1983).

Hoffman, T.A., "Inspiration, Normativeness, Canonicity, and the Unique Sacred Character of the Bible," *Catholic Biblical Quarterly* 44 (1982) 447–469.

Sundberg, A.C., "The Bible Canon and the Christian Doctrine of Inspiration," *Interpretation* 29 (1975) 352–371.

Sundberg, A.C., *The Old Testament of the Early Church* (Cambridge: Harvard University, 1964).

GLOSSARY

Actant—a structural element within a narrative; namely the role fulfilled by a given person or thing in a specific narrative program. An actant is not an actor, for the same actor can fulfill different roles in different narrative programs.

Actantial Model—in the structuralist methodology, this is a model according to which each narrative program in a narrative can be analyzed. This model is comprised of up to six actants (see Fig. 4.9).

Aesthetic Pole—refers to the work of the reader in actualizing a written text. According to reader-response critics, this pole must be working in union with the artistic pole in order for the potentiality of a written text to be reduced to the actuality of a literary work.

Affective Fallacy—concentration of critical attention on the psychological effect of literature on the reader; rejected by the New Critics in their pursuit of objective analysis.

Allegorical Interpretation—a method of interpreting the biblical text that went beyond the literal, historical, physical sense to reach a higher spiritual sense, i.e., the mystery of Christ which is veiled in imperfect formulas.

Allegory—a narrative in which the agents, actions and setting make coherent sense on the literal level but are also systematically symbolic referring to a second, correlated order of agents, concepts and events.

Artistic Pole—refers to the accomplishment of the author of a literary work, i.e., the piece of writing.

165

Canon—(1) any text perceived as having an authority such that an interpreter respects its semantic integrity even when doing so necessitates modifying one's own semantic universe.—(2) the list of texts accepted as authoritative by a faith community.

Canonical Criticism—a methodology which looks beyond the final composition or the final redaction of a biblical book to later points in time when the books were used by a faith community and accepted as canonical. Canonical criticism is more concerned with the accepted text than with the historical processes preceding the text.

Canonical Hermeneutics—involves the study of the historical processes leading to a text, as well as the traditions and sources that eventually became part of the canonical text, but it is most concerned with the manner in which the material functions in the canonical text, i.e., how the material is used and interpreted within the canonical text.

Canonical Process—that process by which a text became part of the life of the believing community, i.e., through repetition and application within the community.

Characters—the persons presented in a narrative work who are interpreted by the reader as being endowed with moral and dispositional qualities that are expressed by what they say and do.

Composition Criticism—a developed type of redaction criticism which stresses the authorial creation of a unified composition rather than the editorial piecing together of pre-existing units.

Connotation (Connotative Aspect)—the range of secondary or associated significances and feelings suggested or implied by a sign (e.g., "home" denotes the place where one lives but connotes privacy, intimacy and coziness).

Conviction—a self-evident truth that belongs to the level of the semantic universe and has the power to function as a condition of the possibility of discourse.

Correlated Sequences—the initial and final sequences or narrative programs in a narrative which, with the intervening topical sequences, constitute the general framework of the deep structure of a narrative.

Criticism—the study concerned with defining, classifying, analyzing and evaluating works of literature.

Cultural Structures—constraints imposed by the culture within which the literary work is created.

Deconstruction—a mode of reading texts which subverts the implicit claim of a text to possess adequate grounds to establish its own structure, unity and determinate meaning. It employs structuralist concepts but undermines the grounds of structuralism by claiming that the more one attempts to find meaning in a text, the more the text deconstructs itself into various other possible meanings.

Deep Structures—formal networks of relations which exist beneath the surface of human social activity (i.e., communication) and which have a uniformity that transcends time and space. These networks of relations, or rules, are the same for all peoples of all times and places, and are discernible in all works of literature.

Denotation (Denotative Aspect)—the primary significance of a sign. That part of the meaning of a sign that is clear, precise, logical and unambiguous because it refers to informational context.

Diachronic Analysis—a methodological approach characterized by its treatment of a phenomenon in terms of temporal process or historical development.

Enlightenment—an intellectual movement developing in the seventeenth century and reaching its height in the eighteenth century which trusted in the ability of human reason to solve the important problems of life, thus freeing man from reliance on authority and unexamined tradition.

Form Criticism—the study of the literary forms of the kinds of material found in the Bible. This methodology is used by critics to identify the primary units which make up the biblical text, enabling them to see how the faith of the early communities shaped the material that entered the Bible.

Hermeneutics—the interpretation of texts including both the formulation of rules governing a valid reading and also exegesis or commentary on the meanings expressed in the text.

Historical-Critical Method—an essentially diachronic method used to analyze biblical texts. It is actually a composite method comprising such distinct methodologies as literary source criticism, form criticism, and redaction or composition criticism.

Humanists—a word coined in the sixteenth century to signify one who worked in fields such as grammar, rhetoric, history, poetry and ethics as distinct from activities less concerned with the moral and imaginative aspects of man such as mathematics, natural philosophy and theology.

Ideal Reader—an aspect of the implied reader wholly defined by the text, each text implying a particular reader with certain competencies and capable of being manipulated in certain ways. The concept of the implied reader involves not only this pre-structuring of the potential meaning by the text but also the real reader's actualization of this potential through the reading process.

Implied Author—the authorial person, distinct from the real author, discoverable in the text. The implied author is responsible for and relatable to the governing values, ideology, concerns and objectives of the text.

Implied Reader—the counterpart of the implied author, the reader required by the text. The implied reader is not, however, an exact counterpart, for this reader is not wholly defined by the text. This reader is the person who by accepting the pre-conditions of the text then, as the aesthetic pole, brings the potentialities of the text to actuality.

Literary Criticism—an expression which, as used by biblical critics, has become a generic term designating any number of critical methodologies borrowed from secular literary critics.

Literary Source Criticism—a methodology which studies how a biblical text came to its present form by means of an analysis of its possible or probable literary sources.

Manifestation—a sign (e.g., a literary text) as it is perceived, i.e., the sign manifesting some of the potentialities of the structures and constraints to which it is subject.

Meaning Effect—a composite effect that results from various levels of meaning that can be discerned in a work of literature (or any other social manifestation) through the use of structuralist methodologies.

Moment of Stabilization—the moment in time when a biblical book (e.g., Isaiah) was redacted or edited for the final time into the form in which it now exists.

Myth—a fantastic story lacking a conscious, logical argument but abounding in symbols. Unlike narratives, whose meaning is derived from the sequential ordering of characters and events, myths derive their meaning from the paradigmatic ordering of symbolic elements.

Mytheme—the fundamental unit of a myth. Each mytheme consists of a certain function linked to a given subject.

Mythical Structures—the patterns or paradigms to which the elements of a myth with symbolic value are ordered and related. Such structures can often be discovered behind and beneath the narrative structures of a given narrative.

Narratee—that fictive entity to whom the narrator of a given narrative tells the story. The narratee is entirely defined by the text and has specific functions that are carried out according to the competencies granted by the implied author.

Narrative—the recounting of a series of facts or events and the establishing of some connection between them.

Narrative Criticism—a form of reader-response criticism used in the study of narratives, e.g., the Gospels and Acts.

Narrative Program (or Sequence)—a unit of the content of a narrative which minimally consists of a subject attributing an object to a receiver.

Narrative Transformation—the alteration of the state of the receiver in a narrative program or sequence. When a subject attributes an object to a receiver, the receiver is then qualified as being in conjunction with the object.

Narrative World—the world of the narration which is a world of finite space and time with a well-defined horizon.

Narrator—the person in a given narrative who tells the story. The narrator is the creation of the implied author, who endows the narrator with certain characteristics and abilities and uses this fictive entity to bring about the artistic effect of the narrative .

New Criticism—a methodology associated with the program announced in John Crowe Ransom's book *The New Criticism* (1941), aiming at scientific objectivity by avoiding both the impressionism of reader oriented criticism and the intentionalism of literary-historical scholarship.

Parable—a short narrative presented so as to stress the connection between the elements of the narration and the lesson it is intended to communicate.

Paradigm—a signifying unit characterized by the systematic ordering of its elements, e.g., a system of values manifested by various narrative elements interspersed throughout the narrative.

Pertinent Transformations—narrative transformations for which there exist opposed transformations within the narrative. These narrative oppositions correspond to oppositions of mythemes.

Point of View—the position from which a story is told, the mode or perspective established by an author by means of which the reader is presented with the characters, actions, setting and events which constitute the narrative.

Pragmatics—the study of the role of the observer (or reader) in the meaning effect of a sign (or literary text).

Reader-Response Criticism—a methodology which maintains that the meanings of a text are the production of the individual reader. Arising in the 1960's, reader-response criticism shifts the perspective from the literary work as an achieved structure of meaning into an activity on the stage of a reader's mind.

Real Author—the real person who wrote a given literary work.

Real Reader—the real person who picks up and reads a given literary work.

Real World Reference—inferences pertaining to the real world which, though evoked by a sign, go beyond the intrinsic meaning of that sign.

Redaction Criticism—a methodology which studies the editorial contribution or the specific theology of the individual biblical writers.

Referential Fallacy—consists in assuming that the conceptual signified of a given narrative is the real world reference and that the elements of that narrative can be interpreted in terms of that reference (e.g., one commits this fallacy by assuming that the Pharisees of Matthew's Gospel refer to the Pharisees of Jesus' day).

Resignification—the process whereby successive communities of faith reinterpret a biblical text according to the interpretive principles implicit in the canonical text itself.

Semantic Square of Opposition—a component of the semantic structure involving three types of relations: contrariety, contradiction and implication (see figs. 4.14–4.16).

Semantic Universe—a system of deep convictions which precede the conscious intentions of an author, and which, by their nature, are unformulatable and can be communicated only indirectly or symbolically. This system of symbolic values is organized by the semantic (mythical) structure.

Semantics—the study of the rules governing the conditions under which signs express meaning.

Semiotics (or Semiology)—the study of the life of signs (including non-linguistic signs) within society; the study of patterned communication in all modalities.

Sign—an element of communication constituted by an inseparable union of signifier and signified.

Signified—that aspect of a sign which is the conceptual reality evoked by the physical signifier (e.g., a red traffic light is the physical signifier which evokes the reality of the need to stop).

Signifier—that physical aspect of a sign which is the immediate object of perception (e.g., a red traffic light, the scent of smoke, or the written marks constituting a literary work).

Structuralism—a methodology that studies the biblical text in terms of recognizable, atemporal and transcultural patterns of thought and experience that are basic to the human condition as such.

Structures—in structuralist analysis, three types of constraints that offer their potentialities to the author's creativity: deep structures, cultural structures and structures of the enunciation.

Structures of the Enunciation—the constraints in a text imposed by the particular life situation in which and out of which a literary composition takes place.

Synchronic Analysis—a methodological approach characterized by its treatment of a phenomenon as constituting a meaningful system at a given time.

Syntactics—the study of the formal system by which a social manifestation operates, e.g., the study of phonemics and grammar in language or the study of narrative structures in narratives.

System of Pertinent Transformations—a system made up of pairs of opposed narrative transformations and organized in the order of the positive narrative development.

Topical Sequences—those narrative sequences occurring between the initial and final correlated sequences that show how various heroes are mandated to reestablish the social order.

Virtual Entity—something which does not yet fully exist, an entity whose full existence depends on its being actualized by some outside agency, e.g., a literary text actualized by a reader.

INDEX